The Wit & Wisdom of WILL ROGERS

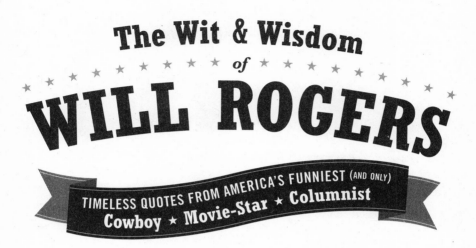

The Wit & Wisdom

of

WILL ROGERS

TIMELESS QUOTES FROM AMERICA'S FUNNIEST (AND ONLY)
Cowboy ★ Movie-Star ★ Columnist

★

EDITED BY
Bryan Sterling

FALL RIVER PRESS

Dedicated to the memory
of Frances Noble Sterling
my ideal partner in life, love, and letters

A Lou Reda Book

Compilation and introductory text © 2009 Mark Wingerson and Suzanna G. Wingerson

This 2009 edition published by Fall River Press.

Microphone illustration © iStockphoto.com
Book design by Suraiya N. Hossain

Fall River Press
122 Fifth Avenue
New York, NY 10011

ISBN: 978-1-4351-0515-7

Printed and bound in the United States of America

10 9 8 7 6 5 4 3 2

 The pages of this book are printed on 100% recycled paper

CONTENTS

INTRODUCTION

The editor of this book, Bryan B. Sterling, died in 2008 before he could complete the manuscript. At his death, he was recognized as the leading authority on the life and works of Will Rogers.

Alone, or together with his wife, Frances Sterling, he published seven books, six concerning Will Rogers: *The Will Rogers Scrapbook, The Best of Will Rogers, A Will Rogers Treasury, Will Rogers in Hollywood, Will Rogers' World,* and *Will Rogers and Wiley Post: Death at Barrow.* He also wrote *Forgotten Eagle,* about Wiley Post, the pioneering aviator who was at the controls of the plane that crashed outside Barrow, Alaska, in 1935, killing him and Will Rogers. Bryan Sterling also compiled most of the material used in *Will Rogers U.S.A.,* the one-man stage show starring James Whitmore; he selected quotations for "Will Rogers Says," a daily syndicated newspaper column that paired the timeless wit and wisdom of Will Rogers with contemporary political events; and he produced an LP recording of Will Rogers's voice.

As Steve Gragert, Director of the Will Rogers Memorial in Claremore, Oklahoma, said at Sterling's funeral service:

> He and Frances have left behind a collection of writings that cannot be replaced, one that anyone in the community of Will Rogers and those beyond can consult with confidence and pleasure.
>
> Sterling and his wife, who died in 2007, were responsible for researching and writing the largest volume of privately published work about the life and words of Will Rogers.

The attraction Sterling felt for this celebrated wit and raconteur was a testament to the universality of Will Rogers's appeal. It would be hard to find two people of more disparate backgrounds. The part-Cherokee Will Rogers was born on a ranch in Oklahoma (known at the time as Indian Territory). Bryan Sterling was born to a Jewish family half a world away in Vienna, Austria, and came to North America as a refugee from Hitler's Third Reich; he learned English in Canada at a British internment camp for enemy aliens.

Bryan Sterling and Will Rogers did, however, have several things in common. They were both largely self-taught men. Will Rogers's formal education ended after two years at the Kemper Military School. As he later said, "I spent two years there, one year in the fourth grade and one year in the guard house. One was as bad as the other." Sterling's formal education ended at age 16, having spent a few years at a college preparatory high school in Vienna.

After his schooling was over, Rogers spent several years wrangling and performing roping tricks in Wild West shows. Sterling started a twelve-year journey by fleeing from Vienna to Prague and then to England, Canada, and finally the United States. Both married strong but supportive wives, had a lively wit, and earned their living through the exercise of an unorthodox entrepreneurial spirit. Both delighted in meeting and getting to know people, were unpretentious, and were generous with their time and money.

When Sterling first learned of Will Rogers, the public memory of him was fading, and Sterling believed he was discovering an unknown rather than becoming aware of a man who, in his prime, was among the most popular and widely recognized in America. Will Rogers became Sterling's life's passion. His interests transcended mere research for books; he and Frances traveled the country to interview people who knew Will; preserving for posterity the recollections of a generation before they passed away. (His interview tapes are now part of the collection of the Will Rogers Memorial.) Sterling counted among his close friends Rogers's sons Will Rogers, Jr., and Jim Rogers; as well as Robert Love, the first manager of the Will Rogers Memorial in Claremore, Oklahoma, his wife Paula MacSpadden Love, and Oklahoma artist Charles Banks Wilson, whose portrait of Will Rogers hangs in the Oklahoma State Capitol.

Bryan and Frances Sterling were honored with the Western Heritage Award in 1983 for their work on *A Will Rogers Treasury,* and the 1997 Will

Rogers Communicator Award for promoting the memory and the message of Will Rogers.

Bryan B. Sterling was married to Frances N. Sterling for fifty-eight years until her death in March 2007. He felt about Fran the same way Will Rogers felt about his wife, Betty: "The day I roped Betty, I did the star performance of my life." In the dedication for *The Best of Will Rogers,* Sterling referred to Frances as "my right arm, my extra pair of eyes, and often my backbone." Although struggling with cancer and other severe medical problems at the time of Fran's death, Sterling was determined to produce one more book about Will Rogers, which he would dedicate to the memory of his beloved wife. This is that book.

It is hard today to overestimate the enormity of the celebrity and star power of Will Rogers during the final phase of his life, 1922 to 1935. He appeared, nay, starred in every medium of his day: print, radio, film, and live performance. His prodigious capacity for work continued during this final period of his life, when he wrote both daily and weekly newspaper columns read by millions, gave weekly radio talks, starred in the *Ziegfeld Follies* Broadway revue, played leading roles in twenty-one talking pictures, published numerous books, and traveled all over the country giving lectures and after-dinner speeches. In addition, he traveled the world as an unofficial "ambassador" for the United States; was a frequent guest at the White House and in the halls of Congress; and a significant contributor to fund-raising for disaster relief efforts, often traveling to the stricken areas. At the time of his death, Rogers was the No. 1 male box office draw in the movie industry and undoubtedly the most popular American in the country. Much has been made of transatlantic aviator Charles Lindbergh's enormous popularity and yet Rogers eclipsed even Lindbergh. The writer and satirist H.L. Mencken noted, with a touch of jealousy, that a word from Will Rogers could make or break any politician. But Will Rogers wore his celebrity lightly and never abused the considerable power it gave him.

Not only did Will Rogers conquer every medium of his time, but in a sense, he invented blogging—the informal, unguarded spontaneity of a blog perfectly mirrors the tone of Will Rogers's newspaper columns. And, indeed, Rogers wrote much as bloggers do today, during breaks between ordinary tasks and whenever the spirit moved him. He would always take with him a little portable typewriter, and when he had a few minutes between takes on a movie shoot, or between performances on Broadway, he would bang out his column and then send it off—typos, misspellings, and all—to the telegraph office.

Will Rogers spoke most often about what the politicians and the government were getting up to, or not, in the "National Joke Factory" as he called Washington, D.C. Having no political ambitions himself, and no formal political affiliation, he was free to comment on the political absurdities of the day regardless of which party or politician produced them. He even set forth the rules he applied to himself with regard to speaking about politics: "An Actor has as much right as any one else to have his Political beliefs . . . but I don't think he should carry any Campaign propaganda into his stage work, either for or against any

Candidate....He has no right to use his privilege as an Actor to drive home his political beliefs....Distribute your compliments and knocks so when the audience go out they don't know where you are politically."

Yet, friendly as he was with politicians, Rogers was quick to spot their hypocrisy. Of Prohibition he wrote:

> They've had a Governor's conference in Washington where they discussed but did not try Prohibition...It was the consensus that there was a lot of drinking going on and that if it wasn't stopped by January that they would hold another meeting and get rid of some more of the stuff.

Will Rogers traveled extensively throughout the world at a time when Americans, for the most part, lived and died in one region of the country without ever traveling beyond. He served both as an unofficial ambassador for America and as the eyes and ears of the folks back home. He sounded the warning early about Hitler. In the late 1920s and early '30s it was not uncommon to hear people praise both Mussolini ("he made the trains run on time") and Hitler ("he put people to work"). In the years before World War II even people as prominent as Charles Lindbergh said complimentary things about the Fascists. Therefore, when Rogers first went to see for himself what Hitler and Mussolini had accomplished in Germany and Italy respectively, he was prepared to be favorably impressed. However, it did not take long for Rogers to take the true measure of those dictatorial leaders.

In 1926, Rogers said that Mussolini was intent on taking over more territory and, although Rogers doubted *Il Duce* would act immediately, he was sure "he will when he thinks they are ready." In fact, Fascist Italy attacked Abyssinia (Ethiopia) in 1935.

Rogers was equally prescient about Hitler. Similarly, he was quick to size up the Japan's aggressive tendencies on the Asian mainland after visiting Japan, Manchuria, and China.

At home, Will Rogers spoke repeatedly about the need for military preparedness. He was particularly incensed about U.S. participation in a Naval Disarmament Conference in the early 1920s that resulted in a commitment by the United States to destroy its newest battleship:

> All the ammunition left over from the war was shot into it and those big guns on the *Texas* they were using, they only are good for so many shots during their lifetime. So we spoiled the Guns of our next-best boat trying to sink the best one.... The Secretary says he don't want the other Nations to know how we did it...Don't worry, they are not going to sink any of theirs...Sinking your own Boats is a military strategy that will always remain the sole possession of America...The other countries sank blueprints.

He was equally concerned about the pitiful state of development of military aviation in America as compared to that of Japan and the great powers of Europe. Rogers believed that the country that had the best air force would have the best chance in the next war and also had a good chance of avoiding being attacked. As he said in late 1926:

> I see where Mr. Coolidge says that if Europe doesn't disarm he will build another airship. Just as well start it...for nobody [in Europe] is going to do any disarming. The way to make them disarm is to start building and quit begging them to disarm.

It is interesting to speculate about how history might have changed had Will Rogers lived until 1941. Would his voice have had the effect of increasing America's military preparedness? Would President Roosevelt's efforts to discourage aggression by Germany have been taken more seriously by Hitler if, at that time, the United States had had a significantly larger military? If military aviation in the United States had been well-funded in the 1930s, would the second and third generation U.S. World War II bombers and fighters have come into production years earlier? Would President Roosevelt have been able, through, the Lend-Lease Act, to provide Britain with aircraft and other weapons to such an increased extent that Britain could have avoided much of the destruction it experienced during the war? Would the United States have had more than three aircraft carriers in the Pacific at the start of the war with Japan? Would they have carried more effective aircraft?

Many of Rogers's observations during the period between the World Wars, though wrapped in his disarming humor and irony, were far more predictive of what was to come than the so-called informed opinions of the statesmen and pundits of the time. President Roosevelt acknowledged as much when he said:

> The first time that I fully realized Will Rogers's exceptional and deep understanding of political and social problems was when he came home from his European trip of 1926. While I had discussed European matters with many others, both American and foreign, Will Rogers's analysis of affairs abroad was not only more interesting but proved to be more accurate than any other I had heard.

If only we had someone today with such clear insight! Perhaps we do. For Will Rogers's wisdom is timeless; applicable, with suitable changes of names and places, to the recurring themes of history and human nature.

—Mark R. Wingerson
Suzanna G. Wingerson

PRESIDENTS

DURING THE FIRST THIRD of the twentieth century Will Rogers easily had more impact on Americans than any other private citizen. His films, daily and weekly newspaper columns, weekly radio broadcasts, and frequent personal speaking engagements established a familial bond between this multimedia superstar and his admirers. It is no surprise to learn that his voice was "heard" everywhere from small villages to the White House. There, President Franklin Delano Roosevelt read Will Rogers's newspaper columns every morning. As James A. Farley, FDR's close friend and two-time campaign manager, explained, "Roosevelt knew that America was reading Will, so he, too, wanted to know just what Rogers had to say each day."

President Woodrow Wilson, a Democrat, was the first President who publicly quoted Will Rogers's humor. Calvin Coolidge, a Republican, invited Rogers to the White House for a weekend, as did the Democrat FDR. Herbert Hoover, a Republican, shared the spotlight with Rogers during a major national broadcast intended to lift America's spirits during the Great Depression.

These remarkable acknowledgments by both Republican and Democratic presidents attest to Will Rogers's political impartiality.

Any man that wants to be President in times like these lacks something.

—February 24, 1933

The only way to keep a Governor from becoming a Senator is to sidetrack him off into the presidency.

—June 1920

Our Civilization is not so hot. Poor Mr. Roosevelt has tried to right some of it. He couldn't do it by persuasion and he can't do it by law, so he may just have to give it up and say, "Boys I have tried to bring a little social justice to you all, but even the Constitution is against me, so back to the old times."

—January 20, 1935

This President business is a pretty thankless job. Washington or Lincoln, either one didn't get a statue till everybody was sure they was dead.

—November 4, 1932

I'll bet you that even Cal Coolidge, who retired at the "peak," wouldn't tell you that worry didn't more than offset the glory.

—November 4, 1932

Coolidge solved his problem better than anybody when he said, "I am for Capital, but I am not against Labor."

In other words: "I love carrots, but I am equally fond of spinach."

—March 30, 1929

In our country every boy is taught that "Every one of you boys have the chance of becoming President, provided you were born in the right part of the country." We are taught that from birth and some of the more feeble-minded ones take it seriously and start preparing by reading what Washington did, and what Lincoln did, and what Teddy Roosevelt did. All of the prospective candidates study what to do, and who to do it to, and then along came Coolidge and did nothing and retired a hero; not only because he hadn't done anything but because he had done it better than anyone.

—March 24, 1929

Mr. Coolidge's vetoing days will soon be over. I bet you the first two weeks he's out of there, in a hotel, when the head waiter hands him a bill, he will mark it "veto" and hand it back.

—February 1929

The Coolidges have a couple of flea hounds there in the White House, and they was feeding the dogs all the time at the table. At one time it looked to me like the dogs was getting more than I was.

One old pup came around to me and I just looked at him and told him, "Listen, my rations won't permit me splitting with you. You are here every day, I am here only once."

—January 8, 1927

A President-elect's popularity is the shortest lived of any public man's. It only lasts till he picks his cabinet.

—December 26, 1928

At the Coolidges in the White House, we had fish that night for dinner...but the next day at lunch—get this!—I was still there at lunch the next day—they had fish hash.

When you are getting down to fish hash, you are flirting with economy.

—January 8, 1927

Hoover is formally into the race now. He is the only candidate in either party by acclamation. The others are candidates by personal desires.

It will be interesting to see what kind of race a known qualified man can make. This election will decide whether qualifications are an asset, or a liability.

—February 13, 1928

My dear Mr. President, I wish you could get off sometime and come to Spain. Other men get their business running so good that they come over here and travel around and see something. It's funny to me that you, with the biggest business in the world can't get men good enough that you can leave it for as long as you want to, and go where you please. That shows right there that you haven't got the right men.

—June 6, 1926

The President goes on the air tonight. Even if he's good, there's plenty of 'em won't like it. He can speak on the Lord's Supper and he will get editorials against it.

America is just like an insane asylum, there is not a soul in it will admit they are crazy. The President being the warden at the present time, us inmates know he's the one that's cuckoo.

—April 28, 1935

Hoover opened his tour of one-niters here tonight. He is breaking in the act that will either get him into the White House, or into the most obsolete circle of all; men who have run for the Presidency.

—August 17, 1928

Mr. Hoover is becoming a typical American President by becoming disgusted with the Senate early in his administration.

Distrust of the Senate by Presidents started with Washington, who wanted to have 'em court-martialed. Jefferson proposed life imprisonment for 'em, old Andy Jackson said, "To hell with 'em," and got his wish. Lincoln said the Lord must have hated 'em, for he made so few of 'em.

Roosevelt whittled a big stick and beat on 'em for six years. Taft just laughed at 'em and grew fat. They drove Wilson to an early grave. Coolidge never let 'em know what he wanted, so they never knew how to vote against him, and Mr. Hoover took 'em serious, thereby making his only political mistake.

—November 1, 1929

ONCE A MAN IS PRESIDENT, HE IS JUST AS **hard to pry** OUT OF THERE AS A SENATOR, OR A TOWN CONSTABLE, OR ANY POLITICAL OFFICER.

—May 29, 1932

The whole show has degenerated into nothing but a dogfight for Vice President. Men, who two days ago wouldn't even speak to a Vice President, are now trying to be one.

—June 13, 1928

Even a glider airplane is not subject to as many conditions as a United States President.

We shouldn't elect a President; we should elect a magician.

—May 26, 1930

Say, that speech by the President yesterday was just about one of the strongest things a President ever said when he said, "Life and property are less safe here than in any other civilized country in the world."

The only difference of opinion we can have about that is, do we come under the heading of "civilized"? I doubt that more than I do the statement.

—April 23, 1929

An awful lot of people are predicting the President's downfall; not only predicting but praying.

We are a funny people. We elect our Presidents, be they Republicans or Democrats, then go home and start daring 'em to make good.

—April 1, 1935

We got to trust somebody to run our country and when we elect 'em, why, let's let 'em alone and see how they do. Then if they don't do, why, throw 'em out when they come up for re-elections.

But always remember this: that as bad as we sometimes think our government is run, it's the best run I've ever seen.

—February 17, 1929

A foreigner coming here and reading the Congressional Record would say that the President of the United States was elected solely for the purpose of giving a Senator somebody to call a horse thief.

—December 19, 1930

Mr. Coolidge's sermonettes are running more to the spiritual than to the political. He has laid off the tariff in favor of faith; and passed up the disarmament treaty in favor of Divine guidance; and sets more store by eternal things than he does by the United States Senate.

He wants us to get back to the old early New England tradition, where if you wasn't praying, you was burning somebody that was.

—July 1, 1930

When will this country that wastes billions on everything finally do justice to a retiring President and allow him for life at least two-thirds of his Presidential salary? It ought to be worth that much to the taxpayer for the privilege we take in crucifying 'em while in office.

—June 5, 1931

Funny thing about us: We will listen to any old shyster politician that comes long to advise, but we just won't trust any of our Presidents when we think they are trying to tell us who to elect.

—September 27, 1930

> **THEY HAVE weeded THE VICE PRESIDENTIAL CANDIDATES DOWN NOW TO JUST THE FOLLOWING: NINETY-SIX SENATORS, 435 CONGRESSMEN AND FORTY-SEVEN GOVERNORS.**
>
> —June 13, 1928

Mr. Hoover was a unanimously popular appointment. Now they find there is a likely chance of him being impeached for treason, indicted for bigamy, and subpoenaed for crossing a boulevard stop.

You give us long enough to argue over something and we will bring you in proof that the Ten Commandments should never have been ratified.

—April 15, 1930

Governments are greatly overrated. The real business of a country is carried on, no matter what King, Emperor, Dictator, or President. We raise all the fuss and mess around over whether it will be a Republican or a Democrat, and 120 million have to make their living under either one.

The whole thing is a lot of applesauce. We have lived under over thirty Presidents. They couldn't have all been great. In fact, if we told the truth about 'em some of 'em was pretty punk. But we drug along in spite of 'em.

—March 8, 1931

Today is our President's fifty-seventh birthday. I look for him to come in for a lot of censure for allowing himself to get that old.

If ever a man should be wished well, it should be him. We think everything has happened to us when nothing has happened to us that we can't look back and see was coming to us.

—August 10, 1931

I have always maintained that no President can be as bad as the men that advise him. We don't need a different man as bad as we need different advisers for the same man.

—August 21, 1932

Wickersham[1] worked two years and spent $2 million, and turned in a report and says, "Now I won't be sure. I can't get the absolute truth, but I think there's a little drinking going on around the country."

And Roosevelt says, "I'll do all that in just three words. Just give me three words." He says, "Let 'em drink." That's all. And he collected $10 million in revenue in the first two weeks, and if he'd had good beer he'd have paid the national debt by now.

—April 30, 1933

Say, this Roosevelt is a fast worker. Even on Sunday when all a President is supposed to do is put on a silk hat and have his picture taken coming out of church, why, this President closed all the banks and called Congress in to extra session—and that's not all he is going to call 'em either if they don't get something done.

—March 6, 1933

Mr. Roosevelt was inaugurated at noon in Washington, and they started the inaugural parade down Pennsylvania Avenue, and before it got halfway down there, he'd closed every bank in the United States.

Now a Republican woulda never thought of a thing like that. No, he'd have let the depositors close it. And mind you, Mr. Roosevelt was just two days ahead of the depositors.

—April 30, 1933

We're wonderful with our Presidents. When the sun is shining we cheer 'em, and let it start raining and if they don't furnish some umbrellas and galoshes, we give 'em the boot right then.

—April 30, 1933

> THEY DO LOVE TO BE PRESIDENT. IT'S THE **toughest** JOB IN THE WORLD, BUT THERE IS **always** 120 MILLION APPLICANTS.
>
> —October 23, 1932

Just sitting here reading in all parts of the papers where so-and-so appealed to the President. Is there nothing that anybody in our country can do themselves anymore? If a strike is even threatened, away goes the "Appeal to the President."

If you must appeal to somebody, appeal to the Supreme Court. That's all they are paid for.

—November 25, 1934

You know, those men go about things different ways. Now
Mr. Hoover didn't get results because he asked Congress to
do something. There's where he made a mistake. This fellow,
Mr. Roosevelt, he just sends a thing up there every morning and
tells them just what they're going to have. Every morning he does
that. Now Mr. Roosevelt, he never scolds them. You know, he kids
them, that's what he does. Congress is really just children that's
never grown up, that's all they are.

—April 30, 1933

I think a Vice President answers about the same purpose as a rear
cinch on a saddle. If you break the front one, you are worse off than
if you had no other.

And speaking of Vice Presidents, will somebody please tell
me what they do with all the Vice Presidents a bank has? I guess
that's to get anybody discouraged before they can see the main
guy. Why, the United States is the biggest business institution in
the world and they only got one Vice President and nobody has
ever found anything for him to do.

—Notes

If we can spare men like Teddy Roosevelt and Woodrow Wilson there
is no sense in any other politician ever taking himself seriously.

—February 22, 1925

The minute it's not raining enough and we can't raise anything, or it's raining too much and we raise too much, we throw our President out and get a new one.

—February 27, 1932

OHIO CLAIMED THEY **was** DUE A PRESIDENT AS THEY HAVEN'T HAD ONE SINCE TAFT. BUT LOOK AT THE UNITED STATES; **they** HAVEN'T HAD ONE SINCE LINCOLN.

—From Notes

Mr. Coolidge handled the thing altogether different. He wouldn't mess with Congress at all. He never messed with commissions either. If the fish wasn't bitin' in the Columbia River, and the Abyssinians wasn't practicin' birth control, Mr. Coolidge never messed with them at all. He just let it go along.

—April 30, 1933

It's a tough life, this being President and trying to please everybody—well, not exactly everybody, but enough to be re-elected.

—September 22, 1929

President Roosevelt is trying to discourage kidnappers. I tell you when Missouri hangs that one that they sentenced, it's going to be a terrible discouragement to one of 'em.

—August 1, 1933

If Mr. Hoover does nothing else but keep our Army and Navy at home, we can forgive him for not giving us rain, lower taxes, and an inflated stock market.

—September 8, 1930

DIPLOMACY

WILL ROGERS WAS NOT IMPRESSED by the formal attire traditionally worn by diplomats for state occasions. He never wore—nor indeed owned—a top hat, tails, or a tuxedo. He simply put on a dark-blue suit to attend even a gala event.

Yet despite his refusal to wear the time-honored uniform of the diplomatic corps, Rogers was never barred from a black- or white-tie dinner. And even without formal diplomatic training, he innately possessed all the qualifications of a most effective emissary. He could travel to countries whose language he did not speak, obtain audiences with government leaders, and often change antagonism to collaboration through his explanations of American attitude. Rogers could joke with Italian dictator Benito Mussolini; play polo with the president of Mexico; interview the king of Spain; visit with

England's presumptive heir to the throne, the Prince of Wales; organize a benefit performance in Ireland for the victims of a disaster; arrange an interview with Adolf Hitler (then change his mind and cancel it); banter with playwright George Bernard Shaw; and travel the width of the Soviet Union to bring back a political and economic analysis of the USSR that Franklin Delano Roosevelt described as more incisive and interesting than any he had ever seen.

Some Americans may view Will Rogers as an entertainer, others as a journalist, but to a whole generation of his countrymen he was an irreplaceable public servant, a diplomat who always knew just the right thing to say.

———

Diplomacy was invented by a man named Webster, to use up all the words in his Dictionary that didn't mean anything.

—June 9, 1928

That's called Diplomacy, doing just what you said you wouldn't.

—June 30, 1929

Diplomacy is a great thing if it wasn't transparent.

—June 6, 1929

I think the only real Diplomacy ever performed by a Diplomat is in deceiving their own people after their dumbness has got them into a war.

—November 10, 1931

DIPLOMATS ARE JUST AS ESSENTIAL TO starting A WAR AS SOLDIERS ARE FOR finishing IT.

—June 9, 1928

You take Diplomacy out of war and the thing would fall flat in a week.

—June 9, 1928

That's why diplomats don't mind starting a war, because it's a custom that they are to be brought safely home before the trouble starts. There should be a new rule saying: "If you start a war while you are your country's official handicap to some other country, you have to stay with any war you start." Then diplomats would begin to "dip."

—July 18, 1929

A DIPLOMAT IS A FELLOW TO KEEP YOU FROM **settling** ON A THING SO EVERYBODY CAN **understand** IT.

—April 28, 1926

The Chinese are the most fortunate nation in the world, for they know that nothing can happen to 'em can possibly be worse than something that's already happened to 'em.

—April 2, 1932

A Diplomat is a man that tells you what he don't believe himself, and the man that he is telling it to don't believe it any more than he does. So Diplomacy is always equal. It's like good bookkeeping: He don't believe you and you don't believe him, so it always balances.

—June 9, 1928

Russia has called home her diplomats from China. China has called home hers from Russia. If they had both done that before the argument was started there would have been no argument.

Our embassy in Japan is the finest one anywhere and I expect as fine as anyone has, even England, who take their Foreign Relations serious. It's a business with them; it's a hobby with us.

—March 5, 1932

Diplomats write notes, because they wouldn't have the nerve to tell the same thing to each other's face.

—June 9, 1928

A Diplomatic Note is like an anonymous letter. You can call a fellow anything you want, for nobody can find out exactly whose name was signed to it.

—June 9, 1928

England has been the Daddy of the Diplomat, the one with the smooth manners. Still going after what he wants, but always a gentleman.

You know, that's one thing about an Englishman, he can insult you but he can do it so slick and polite that he will have you guessing until after he leaves you whether he was friend or foe.

—September 8, 1929

Nowadays we have diplomats to work on wars for years before arranging them. That's so that when it's over nobody will know what they were fighting for. We lost thousands and spent billions, and you could hand a sheet of paper to one million different people, and tell 'em to write down what the last war was for, and the answers that will be alike will be: D——— if I know.

—January 20, 1935

In Diplomacy, the way they work it, they always are careful to not hurt anybody's feelings, but their own people.

—November 1, 1931

The steamship lines must be giving tourist rates to foreign diplomats. There is no other way of accounting for 'em all coming over. Poor Washington, D.C., can't hardly tell what flag to hang out.

—November 17, 1931

That thing Diplomacy…we don't go in so much for that. We train men for everything else. We just wait until we hear of a conference somewhere and send a man or a bunch of 'em, whose only bargaining up to then had been with their grocer, or bootlegger.

—Unpublished article; 1922

When I started on this job, I was expected to tell America's secrets. Well, as we had none, there was no demand from Washington for me to keep them.

You see, there is one thing no nation can accuse us of, and that is secret diplomacy. Our foreign dealings are an open book—generally a checkbook.

—October 21, 1923

DIPLOMATS **meet and eat**, AND THEN RUSH HOME AND WIRE THEIR GOVERNMENT IN CODE THAT THEY FOOLED SECRETARY OF STATE SO-AND-SO.

—June 9, 1928

In this thing called Diplomacy, why, we generally try to pick a man socially equipped so that he won't cut himself while eating. When we have done that, we feel we have succeeded.

—Unpublished article; 1922

We got the most thorough training in every line of business in this country, but statesmanship—that you just decide overnight yourself: I am a statesman.

—November 18, 1934

> # A DIPLOMAT HAS A HUNDRED WAYS OF SAYING **nothing**, BUT NO WAY OF SAYING **something**.
>
> —July 5, 1933

PAPER SAYS: "The new Ambassador arrives in London in a fog."

That's the way all of 'em have arrived and most of them have remained in one.

—January 13, 1924

Diplomats have something called Diplomatic Language—it's just lots of words and when they are all added up, they don't mean anything.

—July 5, 1933

Stay out of Europe, that's a tough game to enter into. Their diplomats are trained; it's their life business. Ours make campaign contributions and wake up in Belgium, and don't know what ocean they crossed to get there. These old diplomats you see sitting around [in Europe], they don't look like much but they out-deal foreigners all their life. What they had to contribute was from their head, not their purse.

—January 19, 1935

The Prince of Wales's marriage is declared off, which means, I suppose, that it will happen; that's generally the type of strategy they always use. That's called diplomacy, doing just what you said you wouldn't.

—June 30, 1929

POLITICS

MOST OF WILL ROGERS'S HUMOR was based on political news reported in local newspapers. Rarely was he seen leaving a newsstand without several different newspapers tucked under his arm. In those days, most cities and towns had at least two newspapers, usually with opposing political positions. Rogers made no secret of his sources. He would begin each of his weekly columns with the confession: "All I know is just what I read in the papers…"

In addition to what he "read in the papers," Rogers traveled extensively in the United States and abroad, gaining personal impressions and views. As he wrote in his column of December 18, 1932: "I read politics, talk politics, know personally every prominent politician. I like 'em and they are my friends but I can't help it if I have seen enough of it to know that there is some baloney in it. I hope

I never get so old that I can't peep behind the scenes and see the amount of politics that is mixed in this medicine before it is dished out to the people as pure statesmanship. Politics is the best show in America and I am going to keep enjoying it."

I tell you folks, all politics is applesauce.

—December 31, 1922

America has the best politicians money can buy.

—*Ziegfeld Follies* routine

Politics has got so expensive that it takes lots of money to even get beat with nowadays.

—June 28, 1931

Ain't it wonderful to have something come up in the country where you can find out just how many political cowards there are.

—March 22, 1931

You know, politicians, after all, are not over a year behind public opinion.

—June 3, 1923

We just have to get used to charging so much off to graft, just like you have to charge off so much for insurance, taxes, or depreciation. It's part of our national existence that we just have become accustomed to.

—November 25, 1934

The trouble with politicians is they see, but they don't see far. They wear reading glasses when they are looking into the future. They got their putter in their hand when they ought to have their driver.

—October 29, 1927

Los Angeles is what is called an average American city; that is the politicians are arguing over where to put their municipal airfield. Each politician is trying to sell the ground that belongs to his friends.

Who ever thought that politics would get into aviation? Say, politics will get into a prairie dog hole if it can sell the ground the hole is on.

—January 21, 1928

Been messing around the country a good deal to find something to talk to you all about. All the politicians are trying to stir up some excitement in their line of work, but I can't find much interest in their graft, outside the ones that are in it.

—May 13, 1928

The best thing I've seen in a political speech was where Chairman Raskob[2] said he had eleven children. That's wonderful. If more men in politics would raise children instead of issues, we would have a bigger and better country.

—October 26, 1928

All I know is just what I get an eye-full of as I wander from tabernacle to tent, preaching a sermon on "Tolerance Toward Politicians."

I try to tell 'em those men are doing the best they can according to the dictates of no conscience. People think I am a paid propagandist, sent out by the politicians just to foster good will toward them. But it's not that at all, it's just that I don't think the politicians are getting what is coming to them. They are lucky.

—April 22, 1928

Politics ain't worrying this country one tenth as much as parking space.

—January 6, 1924

Now about politicians! The least said about them, the best. They haven't the social standing of the diplomats. All of their damage is done internally. Where the ambassador generally winds up with a decoration of red ribbon, the politician generally winds up with an indictment staring him in the face.

—June 9, 1928

NO, IT'S NOT POLITICS THAT IS **worrying** THIS COUNTRY; IT'S THE **second** PAYMENT.

—June 2, 1935

Ain't it funny how many hundreds of thousands of soldiers we can recruit with nerve, but we can't find one politician in a million with backbone?

—February 19, 1929

If you ever injected truth into politics, you have no politics.

—July 15, 1923

Mr. Hoover does one good deed every day. I see where he is going to clean up the Republican organization in the South. That's going to take a little over a day, maybe a day and a half.

The only way that situation can be remedied that I can see, is to ship in some better Republicans from the North, and there just ain't any to spare.

—March 17, 1929

Would like to sell, trade, dispose, or give away to right parties, franchise of what is humorously known as Democratic Party. Said franchise calls for license to enter in national elections; said right, or franchise is supposed to be used every four years, but if intelligent parties had it, they would let various elections go by default, when understood they had no chance.

Could be made to pay, but present owners have absolutely no business with it. Under present management they have killed off more good men than grade crossings have.

—November 7, 1928

The trouble with the Democrats is that they all want to run for President. If they had somebody on that side that would announce he didn't choose to run, why he would be such a novelty that he would be nominated by acclamation.

—September 11, 1927

I am here to explain what the Democratic Party is trying to accomplish, what they are trying to get at. They are trying to get at what few Republicans there are left.

So, a lot of you that have been in doubt all this time as to just what the Democrats were driving at, why, that's it.

—June 10, 1934

Glad to see the Republican Party honor Henry Fletcher.[3] They made him chairman of the Republican National Committee.

'Course, you got to use a little humor when you say it's an honor to hand a man the Republican Party to run at this time.

It's sorter like giving you an empty gun to protect yourself.

—June 6, 1934

The Supreme Court with all its divided knowledge couldn't tell you what either Party stood for.

—September 14, 1928

Party Politics is the most narrow-minded occupation in the world. A guy raised in a straitjacket is a corkscrew compared to a thick-headed Party Politician.

—March 29, 1925

You take a Democrat and a Republican and you keep them both out of office, and I bet you they will turn out to be good friends and make useful citizens, and devote their time to some work instead of 'lectioneering all the time.

—November 11, 1923

> YOU SEE, THE DEMOCRAT IS STILL SO **old-fashioned** THAT HE THINKS POLITICS IS ONE OF THE **honored** PROFESSIONS.
>
> —December 2, 1928

Offers are pouring in for the purchase of the Democrats. All want the title, but no one wants any of the cast.

—November 8, 1928

Politics is a business where most of the men are looking for glory and personal gratification more than they are for money. It's one of the easiest ways of horning into something publicly.

—October 14, 1928

A Democrat will miss supper to explain to you what Jeffersonian Principles are. He don't know what they are but he's heard them spoken of so often that knows no speech is complete without wishing that we'd return to 'em and the only reason that keeps us from returning to 'em is that very reason that we don't know what they were.

—December 2, 1928

If parties are supposed to have to vote together on everything, let each party only send one man from the entire United States. Why pay those others just to be a bunch of sheep?

—March 29, 1925

Politics sure is a gentleman's game. Everybody is of a high type—till the time comes when there is something worthwhile to be little over; then they revert to type.

—October 12, 1928

Look at these politicians here. They are a bunch of local bandits sent by their local voters to raid the public treasury; and if they come home with enough public loot, they are known as statesmen.

—January 12, 1928

You are a politician just in proportion to the loot you have pilfered while in Washington for the old home state. If you can come back with a couple of Boulder Dams, a few government hospitals and jails, and an appropriation to build a road somewhere where nobody lives or wants to, why, if you do all those things you will be putting yourself in line with becoming a statesman.

—August 25, 1929

There is no more independence in politics than there is in jail. I really don't see how anyone can take the whole thing serious— backtracking, all the changing of opinions, all the waiting to see what the majority will be liable to do, all the trading back and forth with each other for support!

They're always yapping about "public service," but it's public jobs that they are looking for.

—November 11, 1928

Children, what was the first thing you learned about politics at school? It was that politics was business, wasn't it? That it was advertised under the heading of "idealism" but it was carried on under the heading of business—and the bigger the business, the bigger the politician.

—October 20, 1929

When a man goes in for politics in England, he has no time to labor and any man that labors has no time to fool with politics. Over there, Politics is an obligation; over here it's a business.

—June 5, 1929

You would be surprised how one bit of political news is so differently construed in different papers. Some public man is a horse thief in one paper; and pick up the other, and he is just about to be canonized and made a saint. Then the next paper will say he is a horse thief in the day, but repents at night.

You can tell in a minute a person that only reads one paper.

—March 17, 1934

The papers just came, having nothing but politics. It does seem that our country could be run much better by someone, if we could only think who.

—September 25, 1932

All you would have to do to make some men Atheists is just to tell them the Lord belonged to the opposition political party. After that they could never see any good in Him.

—March 29, 1925

> **POLITICS IS A GREAT character BUILDER. YOU HAVE TO TAKE A REFERENDUM TO SEE WHAT YOUR convictions ARE FOR THAT DAY.**
>
> —May 29, 1930

I believe a candidate would go over Niagara Falls if he was sure the political wind was with him.

—November 16, 1930

Politics is not the high-class, marvelous thing that lots of you picture. Our whole government workings are crammed with baloney.

But with all the hooey it's the best system there is in the world, and the honesty of our men in big jobs is very high—there is many dumb ones in there, but no downright dishonest ones.

—November 10, 1932

Everything is changing. People are taking their comedians seriously and their politicians as a joke, when it used to be vice versa.

—November 22, 1932

Two-thirds of the men in Politics are not "free born Americans of lawful age and a fair break in intelligence," as the constitution calls for. They was born, but not free; they are of age, but it wasn't lawful; and the break they got in intelligence was not fair.

What I mean is they are just a lot of pawns. They belong to their party and mess around and do odd chores, and do all the dog robbing that is handed out to them to do; then a bunch of men meet in a room and start moving these blocks around. The poor nut don't know if he is to be advanced from an alderman to Senator or sent back to garbage inspector.

—October 14, 1928

Our politics is just a revolving wheel. One party gets in, and through a full stomach and a swelled head it oversteps itself, and out they go. And then the other one gets in and that's all there is to it....

So I guess that's why we got to have two of 'em to keep the other one kind of scared.

—June 24, 1934

CONGRESS

WHEN VISITING WASHINGTON, D.C., Will Rogers would spend much of his time on Capitol Hill. He had friends in both Houses, and in both parties.

He would usually drop in first at the Vice President's office and establish his headquarters there. He would shed his overcoat, hang up his hat, sit down, and talk with the Vice President as only old friends who haven't seen one another for a while do. When it was time for lunch, the two men would walk to the Senate dining room and grab a table. When word spread that Will Rogers was lunching with the Vice President, congressmen and senators surrounded the table to listen and to talk. The atmosphere was genial, with much politicizing and laughter without regard for Party. The fact that the Vice President was having his lunch was no novelty, but that Will Rogers was in the building was a special occasion.

When the Vice President was not in his office, Rogers would simply leave his coat and hat there and go quietly to take a seat in the visitors' gallery of the House. Without drawing attention to himself, he would follow the proceedings. Very soon one of the congressmen would spot him, call for a pause and alert the House that Will Rogers was in the gallery. The Speaker would then welcome the visitor, and his presence would be duly noted in the official record.

———

An Emperor is bigger than a President; he is what a President would be if he didn't have any Congress or Senate to see that he does nothing.

—June 5, 1932

If the President will get up and cuss the Senate and Congress out a couple of more times, he is liable to wake up a hero for never was "cussing Congress" as popular as it is now.

—May 29, 1932

I am to go and perform in the *Ziegfeld Follies* and I have no act. So, I thought I'll run down to Washington and get some material. Now most actors appearing onstage have some writer write their material, but I don't do that; Congress is good enough for me. They have written my material for years and I am not ashamed of the material I have had. You see, there is nothing so funny as something done in all seriousness.

—June 8, 1924

Well, you know how Congress is. They'll vote for anything if the thing they vote for will turn around and vote for them. Politics ain't nothing but reciprocity, you know.

—April 6, 1930

Imagine a Congress that squanders billions, trying to find out where some candidate spent a few thousand?

—June 4, 1920

I wish you could see Rome. They got a lot of things they call forums. They are where the Senators used to meet. I didn't know before I got there that Ancient Rome had Senators. Now I know why it declined.

—Letters, June 5, 1926

Of course Congress is not doing the best they can, but they are doing the best they know how.

—May 29, 1932

When Congress is wrong, we charge it to habit.

—June 30, 1930

An awful lot of people are confused as to just what is meant by a "Lame Duck Congress."

It's like where some fellows worked for you and you let 'em out, but after you fired 'em you let 'em stay long enough so they could burn your house down.

—December 8, 1932

Years ago some fellow in Baltimore left $200,000 for a Presidential retreat. But he left only eighteen months in his Will for Congress to accept or reject it.

Well, Congress can't get the roll called in eighteen months, much less accept or reject anything.

Then, besides, $200,000 wouldn't hardly be enough to pay for the Senatorial investigation to find out where that man got the money that he gave to the country.

—December 23, 1928

There is not a man in the country that can't make a living for himself and his family. But he can't make a living for them *and* his Government, too, not the way this Government is living.

What the Government has got to do is to live as cheap as the people.

—December 21, 1932

I did quite a bit of prowling down in Washington to see what our hired help was doing. They was just appropriating right and left. The U. S. Treasury to them is just a rainbow—there was no end to it.

—March 13, 1932

The Budget is a mythical beanbag. Congress votes mythical beans into it and then tries to reach in and pull real beans out.

—February 24, 1933

They sent the budget to Congress. It took the head man of every department in Washington six months to think up that many figures.

Now you have a budget like you have a limit in a poker game. You're not supposed to go beyond it till at least an hour after the game started. When we do, it just makes another department in Washington.

—December 16, 1928

If we could just send the same bunch of men to Washington for the good of the nation and not political reasons we could have the most perfect government in the world.

—June 6, 1924

Nowadays Mr. Roosevelt just makes out a little list of things every morning that he wants them to do that day (kinder like a housewife's menu list) and for the first time in their lives they are acting like U.S. citizens—and not like U.S. Senators and Congressmen.

—March 17, 1933

[T]he most assuring news of the past couple of weeks was the adjourning of Congress. That wasn't only news; that was an achievement. It looked for a while there the Boys were going to be on our hands from now on. They sure did get rid of a batch of dough, the most money ever appropriated by any Congress, not even excepting war times. All we have to do is make it for 'em and they sure do distribute it.

—March 15, 1931

Wish these newspaper headlines would be more explicit. One says "Senate Adjourns for Rest"—for who?

—Notes

Congress has been getting more money out of us lately than Dillinger.[4] Dillinger don't take it till after you get it, but Congress is making us all sign IOUs for all we will ever get during our lifetime.

—May 13, 1934

I TOLD YOU NOT TO BE TOO OPTIMISTIC ABOUT THE SENATE RESIGNING. THEY FILIBUSTERED ALL LAST NIGHT. WE PAY FOR **wisdom** AND WE GET **wind**.

—May 29, 1931

Congress has had quite a time with the Budget. There's things on there that you had no idea existed. Take, for example, the Department of Justice; it costs us billions of dollars. In fact, Justice is about the cheapest thing we got on our list. Maybe that's why we don't get any more of it.

I'm in favor of paying more for Justice and naming some of the people that ought to have what's coming to 'em.

—December 16, 1928

It is just a day or so before that Congress of ours is supposed to go home. Now whether they do it or not, the Lord himself only knows...[t]here has been better ones than this we couldn't jar loose from. I believe the Rascals meant well this session. They really wanted to help the people, but as usual didn't know how.

—March 8, 1931

Well, all our...Congressmen are away from Washington now. This is the season of the year they do the least damage to their country. They are scattered all over the nation. Some are going to Europe, some even to Turkey. [A] Congressman will go anywhere in the world to keep from going back home and facing his people after the last Congress.

—March 25, 1923

[The Senate] were arguing over some country called Latvia.

Well, if you locked that whole Senate membership up and said, "Not a soul can leave this room until you can tell where Latvia is," say, in years to come they would point out the Senate Chamber as being the place where ninety-six men perished through starvation in the year 1926.

—May 30, 1926

...[it] is going to be mighty tough with no Congress to pick on. I joke about 'em, but you know at heart I really like the Rascals. They are all right. If one wants to do right, our political system is so arranged that he can't do it.

—March 15, 1931

> ...CONGRESS ADJOURNED AT FULL PAY. WHEN DO THE **taxpayers** ADJOURN AT FULL PAY?
>
> —December 26, 1926

Well all I know is just what I read in the papers. And I don't mind telling you that since Congress has adjourned, I am not able to pick up much Scandal. 'Course they left an awful lot of Investigations to be carried out during the summer, for they had to have some place to go. They call it "junketing." That's getting a trip at Government expense. They investigate everything from bird life to pre-historic mammals and radio wavelength.

—March 22, 1931

Mr. Hoover seems to be doing a little better since he got rid of the Gang. A President just can't make much showing against the Mob. They just lay awake nights thinking up things to be against the President on.

—March 22, 1931

[I] just seem lost for comedy since Congress adjourned. I would keep them in session the year round for my business but I have some consideration for the rest of the people, so I sacrifice my needs for the good of the country.

—Lecture, March 1925

Did you see where this new Senator says he is going to use "Common Sense in the Senate?" That's what they all say when they start in. But if nobody understands you, why, you naturally have to switch.

—January 27, 1924

Congress meets tomorrow morning. Let us all pray: Oh Lord, give us the strength to bear that which is about to be inflicted upon us. Be merciful with them, Oh Lord, for they know not what they're doing. Amen.

—December 5, 1926

Congress is so strange...a man gets up to speak and says nothing...nobody listens...and then everybody disagrees.

—Ziegfeld Follies routine, 1918

I see there is a bill up in Congress now to change the Constitution... It means the men who drew up this thing years ago didn't know much and we are just now getting a bunch of real fellows who can take the old parchment and fix it up like it should have been all these years....Now when they get the Constitution all fixed up, they are going to start in on the Ten Commandments, just as soon as they find somebody in Washington who has read them.

—December 13, 1922

Washington, D.C., papers say "Congress is deadlocked and can't act!" I think that is the greatest blessing that could befall this country.

—January 27, 1924

I see where they introduced a bill to raise Senators' and Congressmen's salaries....Looks like with Congress charging more, the people are getting harder to displease then they used to be.

—March 22, 1925

They are going to limit debate in the Senate. It used to be that a man could talk all day. Now, as soon as he tells all he knows, he has to sit down.

[This] Congress will be composed of…what is known as "Lame Ducks." That's a man who has been defeated and still holds office. There is no other business in the world that allows a man to work after he is fired, except politics.

—November 16, 1924

ABOUT ALL I CAN SAY FOR THE… SENATE…IS THAT IT **opens** WITH A PRAYER, AND **closes** WITH AN INVESTIGATION.

—Notes

You see they have two of these bodies, Senate and…House. That is for the convenience of visitors. If there is nothing funny happening in one, there is sure to be in the other, and in case one body passes a good bill, why, the other can see it in time, and kill it.

—June 8, 1924

I see where Congress has just asked [to appropriate money] to put a new roof on and redecorate the White House. So you see it was kind of a trade. The President was tired of moving his bed every time it rained and he figured if I do right by these Boys, they will do right by me.

Then again there is liable to be a Presidential raise coming up any time and those are the Boys who have to okay it.

The principal bad feature is that it will make more men want to hold office, and once a man wants to hold public office he is absolutely no good for honest work.

—November 23, 1924

Most of them birds will just be getting up and nodding now, why, a third of them won't be able to answer roll call.

—Lecture, March 1925

DEMOCRATS AND REPUBLICANS

"I AM NOT A MEMBER of any organized political party—I am a Democrat" is the answer Will Rogers supposedly gave when asked about his political affiliation. Later he wrote that, as a humorist, he ought to allege Democratic affiliation because it seemed to him the more humorous party.

The fact that Will Rogers's political inclination is still hard to pinpoint shows that he spoke and wrote without bias. That he seemed to pick on one or the other party at different times merely demonstrates that he could give an account of events without injecting his personal preference.

Rogers's prolific output—two million words in print and many more millions spoken in years on the lecture circuit, not to mention his after dinner speeches and radio broadcasts—never alienated listeners because of perceived partisanship. Rogers's political friendships extended to both sides of the political aisle and no hint of any partisanship was ever even alleged. Elected officials were happy to be photographed with Will Rogers, and while Rogers did not endorse candidates, his picture with politicos often appeared in campaigns and was thought to be most helpful.

Since voting is a strictly private matter, Rogers did not discuss it, however it is known that on Election Days he was rarely at his primary residence in Pacific Palisades, California: indicating, perhaps, that Will Rogers may not have voted.

Anyone can be a Republican when the Stock Market is up, but when stocks are selling for no more than they are worth, I tell you, being a Republican—it's a sacrifice.

—Broadcast, October 14, 1934

During all this campaigning, a dozen Presidential candidates couldn't make any more headway than a preacher that didn't talk politics.

—October 19, 1928

The Democrats were a kind of semi-heathen tribe. They were what you'd call a nomad race and they would live on little because they had nothing else—but they don't live on little when they get in office—don't forget that.

—June 24, 1934

To be a Democrat you have to be an optimist; and you've got to have a sense of humor to stay one.

—Notes

I see by today's paper where Senator Borah[5] made an appeal to the country to donate a dollar or more to save the respect of the Republican Party.

I just mailed $5 to make five Republicans respectable.

—March 12, 1928

I received my $5 back from Senator Borah that I sent him to clean up five Republicans. He wasn't able to raise the funds because people realized that it was a lost cause. You can't make the Republican Party pure by more contributions, because contributions are what got it where it is today. That was a noble idea of Borah's but noble ideas don't belong in politics.

—April 16, 1928

The only way in the world to make either one of those old Parties look even halfway decent is to keep them out.

—November 11, 1923

Lots of people never know the difference between a Republican and a Democrat. Well, I will tell you how to tell the difference.

The Democrats are the ones who split. That's the only way you can tell them from the Republicans. If the Democrats never split in their lives, there would be no such thing as a Republican.

—August 16, 1925

The Republicans have always been the party of big business, and the Democrats of small business. The Democrats had their eye on a dime, and the Republican on a dollar.

So you just take your pick.

—April 22, 1928

So many Republicans have promised things and then didn't make good that it's getting so that a Republican promise is not much more to be depended on than a Democratic one. And that has always been the lowest form of collateral in the world.

—July 22, 1923

Of all the comical things, the so-called Party Leaders take the cake. The Democratic leaders have assured their man that he will carry every state he has gone into. The Republicans have told their man that he was a cinch for everything east of the Golden Gate and a chance for a split in Honolulu.

If either candidate believes one-half of one percent what any of his henchmen say, then neither one is smart enough to be President.

—October 22, 1928

The difference between a Republican and a Democrat is that the Democrat is a cannibal; they have to live off each other, while the Republicans live off the Democrats.

—Notes

Don't blame all the things that have happened to us lately on the Republicans—they're not smart enough to have thought 'em up.

—Notes

Republicans have a certain foresight and would take over the reign of government about the time things were going good. And when they saw pestilence and famine was about to visit on the land, they would slip it back to the Democrats.

—June 24, 1934

If we didn't have two parties, we would all settle on the best man in the country and things would run fine. But, as it is now, we settle on the worst ones and then fight over 'em.

—January 17, 1932

YOU KEEP A REPUBLICAN GETTING **interest** ON HIS MONEY AND HE DOESN'T CARE IF IT'S STALIN OF RUSSIA WHO IS **doing** IT.

—March 26, 1933

A Democrat is just an alarm clock; he wakes you up, but you don't necessarily have to get up.

—*"How to be Funny"*

A flock of Democrats will replace a mess of Republicans. It won't mean a thing. They will go in like all the rest of 'em; go in on promises and come out on alibis.

—September 14, 1930

The trouble with the Democrats has been that up to now they have been giving the people what they thought they ought to have, instead of what they wanted.

—March 30, 1929

That's one peculiar thing about a Democrat; he would rather have applause than salary. He would rather be told that he is right, even if he knows the guy is a liar, than he would to know he is wrong, but belongs to the Republican Party.

—September 22, 1929

> THE DEMOCRATS ARE INVESTIGATING **slush** FUNDS. IF THEY CAN FIND OUT WHERE IT COMES FROM, THEY WANT THEIRS.
>
> —June 4, 1920

The Republicans want a man that will lend dignity to the office, and the Democrats want a man that will lend some money.

—July 11, 1930

I generally give the party in power, whether Republican or Democrat, the more digs because they are generally doing the country the most damage. And besides, I don't think it's fair to jump too much on the fellow that's down. He is not working; he's only living in hopes of getting back in on the graft in another four years, while the party in power is drawing a salary to be knocked.

—November 9, 1924

Seems funny me up here telling all this Democratic thing. You know any big company is owned by Republicans, I said, "How about it here? I'm going to get up and naturally say something complimentary about the Democrats."

So they told me, "Well, it's all right, Will. We'd rather have been saved by a Republican, but we will take a Democrat anyhow."

—April 30, 1933

The Democrats are having a lot of fun exposing the Republican campaign corruption, but they would have a lot more fun if they knew where they could lay their hands on some of it themselves for next November. The difference in corruption in the two parties was seven million votes last election, so the Democrats have got to investigate and find out how to improve their corruption.

—March 15, 1928

I really can't see any advantage of having one of your own Party in as President. I would rather be able to criticize a man than to have to apologize for him.

—March 18, 1923

You can't train a Democrat. He acts like he is trained, but he ain't; most of that devilment he just comes by naturally.

But dissatisfaction is his stock in trade. He knows the Republicans are sharpers, but [Democrats] don't know enough to prove it on 'em; and the Republicans know that they are sharpers and know that the Democrats will never know enough to prove it on them.

—March 24, 1929

I belong to neither Party…. Both parties have their good and bad times, only they have them at different times. They are each good when they are out, and each bad when they are in.

—May 1, 1926

How often do politicians say, "I don't have to tell you what our great party stands for! You know the facts! We rely on your intelligence!"

About the only thing that you can safely say is that both parties stand for re-election!

—September 21, 1928

The Republican candidate says "The majority of the country is prosperous." He means by that that the Republicans are prosperous, and he kinder insinuates that if a man don't know enough to be a Republican then how can he expect to know to be prosperous?

—October 28, 1928

There is something about a Republican that you can only stand him just so long; and on the other hand, there is something about a Democrat that you can't stand him quite so long.

—November 9, 1932

The Democrat candidate says the country is not prosperous. He means of course by that, that the Democratic end of the country is not doing as well as they could if they were in office. There is a great many Democrats who are forced to earn a living by the sweat of their brow, when all they [want to] be doing is endorsing a government paycheck.

—October 28, 1928

Everybody is always asking "What's the matter with the Democratic Party?"...The only thing wrong with it is the law killed it. It won't let a man vote but once, and there just ain't enough voters at one vote each to get it anywhere.

—January 19, 1929

Things must be in a pretty bad way in the Republican Party when they have only two men who think they are good enough to run. Why, the Democratic Party, they have a thousand who think they are good enough.

According to that, the Democrats must have the most able party.

—June 9, 1924

I don't know why it is, but Democrats just seem to have an uncanny premonition of seizing up a question and guessing wrong on it. It almost makes you think sometimes it is done purposely. You can't make outsiders believe it's not done purposely. For they don't think people could…make that many mistakes accidentally.

—January 19, 1929

ELECTIONS

WILL ROGERS WAS BORN ON ELECTION DAY in 1879. As he said, "That's why I have always had it in for politicians."

The circus of American elections was a mainstay of Rogers's humorous quips, however his opinion of the electoral process was much more complicated than his down-home language implied. Certainly he decried corruption, the mendacity of the process, and the generally weak character of the politicians running, but his extensive world travels tempered his judgment. He understood, as did Churchill, that democracy was an extremely messy and inefficient system, yet it was superior to any other type of government.

Will Rogers covered every presidential convention from 1924 to 1932, and he once quipped: "No one can possibly do anything to mar the dignity of a convention. The whole thing is applesauce."

Nevertheless, they were addictive. "It's a great game this convention game. I don't suppose there is a show in the world with as much sameness in it as it has got. You know exactly what each speaker is going to say, before he says it; you know before you go who will be nominated; you know the platform will always be the same—promise everything, deliver nothing. You cuss yourself for sitting day in and day out looking at such nonsense. But the next four years find you back there again."

Once Rogers was asked to speak in favor of a candidate at a rally. Because the request came from someone he felt he could not refuse, he agreed to do it. "[T]his is my first crack at a political speech and I hope it flops," Rogers explained to the audience. "I don't want it to go over [well] and then have to go into politics, because up to now I have always tried to live honest." About the candidate, he said, "[He] is quite a novelty…one of the few men that didn't go into politics through necessity. He was wealthy when he started. He went into politics to protect it, for they say there is honor among thieves." The candidate sat stone-faced through Rogers's speech, possibly because, as Rogers later noted, "The poor fellow don't know yet whether I am for him or against him!"

Did you read [the] Senator['s]...appeal this morning to the Republican Party to "please clean up before [the] election?" He intimated that they could get back to normal after [the] election but to kinder lay off till some of this has blown over. Now that's not an unreasonable demand to make of a party—to remain decent one year in four.

—March 19, 1928

They talk about what a great thing the radio has been for politicians and candidates. Why, there has been more people got wise to over the radio than Senate investigations have exposed.

Nothing in the world exposes how little you have to say as radio.

—March 30, 1929

In most places it's awfully hard to get folks to go and register to vote, but here in Los Angeles, where we do everything "big," why, each qualified voter is allowed to register himself and ten dead friends. If he hasn't got ten dead friends, why, he is allowed to pick out ten live ones, just so they don't live in this state.

The Republicans are kicking on this arrangement, as they claim that system of registration gives the Democrats the best of it, as very few Republicans have ten friends.

—October 17, 1934

Dissatisfaction is what makes a Democrat. It's not environment when we start out trying to make everybody have "moral" elections, why, it just don't look like we going to have Marines enough to go round. 'Course we don't need 'em here at home.

—May 26, 1928

I believe a man should be allowed to spend as much as he can to be elected. Deliver us from a cheap Senator. No man can ever rise above his surroundings and if you put a man in that was elected on nothing but campaign speeches, you are going to have nothing but wind to represent you.

—December 26, 1926

Corruption is something that has always been going on. These deals gradually come under the heading of legitimate campaign business. If you promise a man that if you are made Senator that he will be made a judge, why, you have sold him something; his votes have helped you to get your salary.

You might promise him a river to get a dam built on, but you have promised him something directly or indirectly, and you can't get the voters to distinguish the difference—if there is any.

—April 22, 1928

The idea of closing a bank of your own free will and accord is as foreign to a Republican as selling stock you don't own is foreign to a Democrat. It's not that the Democrat's conscience would hurt him, it's just that he never thought of it.

—March 26, 1933

We got our elections going along on a pretty good basis. We don't regulate 'em by morals, we regulate 'em by supply and demand. Now this year I think will be a good year. I think votes ought to bring more than they ever did.

—May 26, 1928

Election is here in a couple of days and a lot of people lose a lot of sleep and get all heated up over it, and politicians will spout off to you that if such and such is elected, that will mean sure destruction of the whole country.

The Republicans are not going to start poisoning all the Democrats. The Democrats wouldn't just send the Republicans into the front line trenches in case of war. I don't think we will be ruined, no matter who is elected, so the politicians will have to wait four more years to tell us who will ruin us then.

—November 2, 1924

It *must* be getting near election time; they have commenced taking up all the babies and kissing them.

—July 8, 1923

Who cares nowadays who is elected to anything? They are not in office three days till we realize our mistake and wish the other one had got in. We are a nation that runs in spite of, and not on account of our government.

—May 29, 1926

I see by the papers this morning that each political party has some plan of relieving the unemployed.

They have been unemployed for three years, and nobody paid any attention to 'em. But now, both parties discovered that [although] they are not working, there's nothing in the Constitution to prevent them from voting.

—June 6, 1932

The next election looks like a Democratic year. It's two years away. That's the main reason it looks like a Democratic year. Any [year] two years away always looks like a Democratic year. Democratic politics are what you might call future politics.

—September 19, 1926

With an election coming on, I want to draw your mind off of golf as much as I can and onto the big issues of the day. But it's awful hard to get people interested in corruption unless they can get some of it....People just figure "Well, there couldn't be so much corruption, or some of it would have come my way." And the fellow that has received any of it, naturally he is in favor of a continuation of the policy.

—April 22, 1928

This is not election about parties or policies this fall; it's an election where both sides really need the work. In fact, I think if you would split the salaries between every two candidates running, they would call off the election.

—August 1, 1932

Well, today they are voting on...whether to keep a governor two years or four. I think a good honest governor should get four years and the others life.

—November 8, 1927

I know part of the Presidential candidates personally—well, I know about eighteen or nineteen of them. The others I know by reputation.

—May 25, 1924

You can have famine, heel flies, and an epidemic of the itch, all through the first three years of a political reign, and then kinder pick up on the last year, and you can walk in. No voter can remember back a year. What happened in the last six months is as far as his mind can grasp.

—March 30, 1929

It's really remarkable what the politicians think of us every four years. Their every thought is of us every fourth fall.

—October 5, 1924

NO ELECTIVE CANDIDATE IS EVER AS **bad**, OR AS **good**, AS WE EXPECT HIM TO BE.

—September 16, 1934

If I was running for office I would rather have two friends in the counting room than a Republican slush fund behind me.

—November 9, 1924

Elections are a good deal like marriages; there is no accounting for one's taste. Every time we see a bridegroom, we wonder why she ever picked him, and it's the same with public officials.

—May 10, 1925

When you regulate the price that a man can spend for votes, you are flirting with the very backbone of American liberty. If we can't be a good nation, let's at least not be accused of being a cheap nation.

—May 20, 1926

They say it's wrong to "buy" votes, but you notice from the election returns that the fellow that "bought" the most got elected. A bought vote is better than no vote at all. The counter can't tell whether they are bought, or just bargained for.

—November 4, 1926

Both sides just spent the whole summer hunting up things to cuss the other side on. That the other side might be right in a lot of things never entered their head. In fact, they wouldn't let it enter it. A politician is not as narrow-minded as he forces himself to be.

—October 30, 1932

You can't get people to throw another man out just because you want his job. You got to promise the people something, even if you don't ever expect to give it to them.

—October 29, 1927

It don't take much political knowledge to know that a man can get more votes running on the people's request, than he can running on his own request.

—August 3, 1927

Candidates have been telling you that if elected they would pull you from this big hole of financial misery. Now is a good chance to get even with 'em, just to prove what a liar they are.

—November 2, 1930

Tomorrow is another Primary Day. In the old days, when Senators were Senators, why, the State Legislature would pick out the ones that were to run, now they pick themselves.

You put an ad in the paper, saying: I believe that I am needed! Maybe it's an original idea with you, but there is no way to keep you from running. There is no qualification necessary.

—August 11, 1930

Before you know it there will be another election along to pester us. But the whole thing will mean nothing in our lives. All we do is just dig up their salary and they all get the same price, Republican or Democrat. So, there is no way we can win.

—October 12, 1930

PERSONALLY I THINK THIS IS THE RIGHT YEAR FOR A **good** MAN TO BE DEFEATED IN.

—November 2, 1930

Oklahoma and Texas [Democrats] have an original primary system. [We] have so many seeking office that the first primary is only to find out how many are desirous of living off the State. The second primary is to eliminate fifty percent of these. The third primary is to get rid of half of what is left. The fourth is to eliminate any good man that might have crept in by mistake. Now you have just politicians, so the fifth one is to leave in the two worst, and they run it off [in the last primary].

—July 30, 1930

Anything important is never left to the vote of the people. We only get to vote on some man; we never get to vote on what he is to do.

There is things about it that is not just exactly 100 percent kosher.

—April 30, 1932

Al Smith told exactly what his ideas were on every question. No wonder he can't be elected. Imagine a man in public office that everybody knew where he stood. We wouldn't call him a statesman; we would call him a curiosity.

—March 1, 1933

Take your campaign contribution and send it to the Red Cross and let the election be decided on its merits.

—September 21, 1928

That's the trouble with a politician's life—somebody is always interrupting it with an election.

—1922

Every man looks good until he is elected.

—Bull Durham ad, 1925

WAR AND PEACE

WILL ROGERS WAS A MAN OF PEACE, though he was convinced that wars in Europe and against Japan were imminent. He felt that while America slept, its future enemies were preparing for the fight to come. He tried to warn his generation, urging that it arm, recruit, and fully equip the Army and Navy, strengthen the Marine Corps, and above all, build a large Air Force. He spoke and wrote in defense of Colonel Billy Mitchell, and attended his court-martial. Will Rogers believed, as did the Colonel, that Japan would attack the United States, and that the attack would be made on Hawaii's Pearl Harbor. Neither farsighted American would live to see the disastrous fulfillment of their warnings.

Rogers had another great vision, which he expressed to a studio audience following a transcontinental radio broadcast on March 31, 1935. Even though the show was over, the studio audience was reluctant to leave. So Rogers obliged them with an account of his visit to Washington, D.C., earlier that week. Like all of Rogers's broadcasts, the remarks were unscripted, but because the program was recorded in the control room, a tape of his comments to the audience exists, and they demonstrate his clear thinking and plainspoken wisdom. He said:

"You know, Nye[6] that runs all this ammunition thing. And I don't think I'm betraying any confidence when I tell you that Mr. Nye tells me that out of this ammunition thing they're going to introduce a new bill to take the profits out of war. And he assured me that they was gettin' it ready and that they was going to have it ready in a few days. And, so he said that's what they was going to do. They're gonna put in a bill where in case there is a war that nobody will be allowed to make any profit from it. And I think that's a great idea, and I know everybody does. I think it would be still a better idea and would keep us out of a lot of war if they put in the bill in there that not only couldn't we make any out of our own war, but we couldn't make any out of anybody's war. If we knew we couldn't sell anything to any other nation while they was at war, we'd never get in it. That's just a little idea of mine.

That ain't in the bill. Too much sense to that to ever get in the bill.
I know that."

Thank goodness there will be no more wars. Now you tell one.

—January 6, 1927

Celebrated twelve years continuous peace yesterday, and we
looked as bad off as we did twelve years ago when we celebrated
the end of two years of war.

If we pulled together as much to put over a siege of peace as do
a spell of war, we would be sitting pretty. But we can't hardly wait for
a war to end to start taking it out on each other.

Peace is like prosperity; there is mighty few nations that can
stand it.

—November 12, 1930

I told the Secretary of our Navy right from the stage, that I wished
we had the biggest Navy in the World, the biggest Army, and the
biggest Aeroplane force, but have it understood with the taxpayers
that they are *only to be used on the home grounds.* Now how in the

world will you tell me is there a better way to prevent war than that. Be ready for it and stay at home. When they know they can't lick you they certainly are not coming away over here to try it.

—May 5, 1929

If America don't look out they will be caught in the next war with nothing but a couple of golf clubs. You see, in the next war you don't want to look out, you want to look *up*. When you look up and you see a cloud during the next war to end wars, don't you be starting to admire its silver lining till you find out how many Junkers and Fokkers are hiding behind it.

—December 4, 1926

Talk about stopping war. I will bet any man in the United States five thousand even that there ain't a man in this country that can draw up a bill that the Senate themselves won't go to war over while they are arguing it.

—July 22, 1923

The League of Nations to perpetuate peace is in session. On account of Spain not being in the last war, they won't let her in. If you want to make peace you have to fight for it. Yours for peace without politics.

—September 3, 1926

You see they're rushin' around now, signing up. Just like a baseball team. You know, all of Europe—they don't know who's going to be partners in the next war, so everybody's rushin' around to get some new signatures on the thing.

I bet Dillinger didn't have as much trouble signing up his gang as some of them over there do.

—March 31, 1935

IT'S **cheaper** FOR US TO FIGHT A NATION THAN TO **confer** WITH THEM.

—Unpublished article, 1922

We get into more things for less reasons than any nation in the world. Not long ago Nicaragua, they was havin' some trouble, they just wanted to have a good time down there among themselves and put on a little civil war and just use home talent; they didn't want no outsiders at all, just take up a few among their own people. Do you think they could have a little war, have their little fun? No, we was right there; we had to be there.

—April 6, 1930

When the nations quit fightin' they had nothing to do, so they started in to confer and it's always been a matter of doubt as to whether the fightin' wasn't better than the conferrin' is. In fact I know it is with us, we had more friends when we was fightin' than we have now since we started in, into conferrin'.

—April 6, 1930

They're rushin' around, saying "Who'll help out?" And they'll be coming over here with their propaganda pretty soon. You know, there'll be delegations come and say, "We didn't come to persuade you or anything, but in case civilization is attacked, why, where do you boys stand?"

Well, we better tell 'em, "Well, if civilization hasn't done any more than it has since the last war, why we're against it. So we'll just stay with the side that's against civilization. We tried it the other way last time."

—March 31, 1935

You know, you can be killed just as dead in an unjustified war, as you can in one protecting your own home. We lost lots of fine men down there [Nicaragua], for what? To make [their] elections as pure as Chicago's?

—May 26, 1929

It always helps out in your recruiting and your patriotism if you can make your own people believe you were the one pounced on.

—November 10, 1931

I think, without any degree of egotism we can say, with our tremendous resources, we can lick any nation in the world single-handed, and yet we can't confer with Costa Rica and come home with our shirts on. You know, we mean well when we go into these conferences, we don't go over there to try to put it over on anybody or we don't go into wars to get anything out of it, we go in with the best intentions in the world.

—April 6, 1930

Haiti, just the other day wanted to have a little shootin' and use each other as targets. Well, the day the shootin' was to come off, before they could fire the opening overture we was there, we was right there to get in it. We not only sent the Marines down, we sent a commission down, too. The Haitians they don't mind Marines because they have been around these countries and they are likable chaps, but they told them, "For the Lord's sake send this commission home; we will do anything if you send this commission home."

—April 6, 1930

A funny thing about us, we never was very good in conferences. We are great talkers but we are mighty poor conferers, you know. America has a unique record. We never lost a war and we never won a conference in our lives.

—April 6, 1930

Awful lot of war talk now, but war is kinder like [our] California sunshine; the more you talk about it, the less you get.

—Not identified

> I AM A **peace** MAN. I HAVEN'T GOT ANY USE FOR WARS AND THERE IS NO MORE **humor** IN 'EM THAN THERE IS REASON FOR 'EM.
>
> —December 4, 1931

We thought the late big war was the worst thing that could possibly happen—nothing compared to what the peace terms have inflicted on the people.

—Notes

[If you want to stop wars, consider drafting capital.] When the millionaire knows that you are not only going to come into his office and take his secretary and clerks, but, that you come in to get his dough, there wouldn't be any war. Take all he has, give him a bare living, the same as you do soldiers.

—June 10, 1923

I like this part of [the President's] message best: "Both parties in Nicaragua were pleased with the outcome of their election and have asked for the Marines again next time. But I did not commit myself."

Yes, I think we could let [the President] contract for that one. The Marines will certainly be tickled to know that they can get booking four years ahead. They have always just had to pick up little wars from day to day. Now they can kinda look ahead and plan, and have a permanent address.

—December 4, 1928

England, France, and Germany have diplomats that have the honor of starting every war they have ever had in their lifetime. Ours are not so good—they are amateurs—they have only talked us into one.

—June 9, 1928

You can have all the advanced war methods you want, but, after all, nobody has ever invented a war that you didn't have to have somebody in the guise of soldiers to stop the bullets.

—May 12, 1928

Peace is like a beautiful woman—it's wonderful, but has been known to bear watching. So when you are having tea [with those boys discussing disarmament] let's hold out a rowboat at least.

—November 3, 1929

That's one mightily satisfying thing about our country. Our young men can get us ready for wars faster than our diplomats can talk us into them.

—April 13, 1930

Wars are just like depressions, they come when you least expect 'em.

—November 8, 1931

A lot of the prominent men have been hollering about taking the profit out of the next war. They are always talking about it but they never passed a bill, did you notice that?

—May 26, 1935

I would rather have a nation declare war than peace against me; in a war you know who your enemies are. But in peace you don't know either friend or foe.

—Notes

They are talking of having another war, just as soon as they get it straightened out who won the last one.

—Notes

THOUGHT THE ARMISTICE TERMS [WOULD] READ LIKE A **second** MORTGAGE, BUT THIS READ LIKE A **foreclosure**.

—The Cowboy Philosopher on the Peace Conference

I believe it is a record. Japan and China have been fighting now for one solid week and we haven't entered our Marines. What's the matter, are they barred? Maybe they are eliminated on account of being professionals.

—May 11, 1928

These unofficial invasions are just like a man going to dinner where he was not invited. Now he may have come unofficially, but still he eats just as much as if he had been invited.

—January 21, 1923

I tell you, wars will never be a success, until you do have a referee, and until they announce just what it's for, before they start, and then, at the end, say who is the winner, and just what does he win.

—January 21, 1931

Trace any war that ever was and you will find some nation was trying to tell some other nation how to run their business.

—June 28, 1925

When the big countries quit meddling, then the world will have peace.

—August 9, 1933

Say, are you surprised at all the war talk you hear?

If we are out upholding downtrodden nations, it will take a bookkeeper to keep track of our wars.

—February 18, 1932

[A] Senator…wants a conference to decide "your rights on the seas, during a war which you haven't yet been able to get into."

That is just like holding a convention to discuss "the rights of [an] innocent bystander during a fight between police and bandits."

He only has one right and that's the right to a decent burial.

—January 30, 1929

All our highly civilized nations are great humanitarians, but if two countries are going to kill each other off, neutrals at least would like the privilege of furnishing the ammunition.

When judgment day comes, civilization will have an alibi: "I never took a human life, I only sold the fellow the gun to take it with."

—July 15, 1929

When you get into trouble 5,000 miles away from home, you've got to have been looking for it.

—February 9, 1932

We haven't got any business in these [Asian] wars. Seven thousand miles is a long way to go to shoot somebody, especially if you are not right sure they need shooting, and you are not sure whether you are shooting the right side or not.

—May 1, 1932

Hoover is [visiting] Nicaragua. He wants to see some of our Marines. He hasn't seen any since the old days in China. If it wasn't for the movie weeklies picturing them going from one country to another, we would never know what they looked like.

—November 22, 1928

I HAVE A **scheme** FOR STOPPING WAR. IT'S THIS: NO NATION IS ALLOWED TO ENTER A WAR TILL THEY HAVE **paid** FOR THE LAST ONE.

—August 29, 1928

I just suggest that the reason France says it's wrong to fight us is because we may have more cruisers than they do? Now, this is only a suggestion and it may not be based on facts, but perhaps if we had more cruisers than England they, too, might sign a treaty saying, "War is wrong with you people."

—December 21, 1928

WOMEN

THERE IS NO BETTER or more complete way to introduce this subject than the words of Rogers himself, from April 23, 1928:

> Here in New York, Tammany Hall, the local political machine is just a bunch banded together under a Constitution, which says, "Get these Jobs and stay with 'em, and if the time ever does come when you have to give it up, give it up to another Tammany man."
>
> Well, the first time they had a meeting to elect a Leader, why, the women come in and wanted to vote. Well the men had never considered that, they had forgotten about the Nineteenth Amendment[7] on account of being so busy thinking about the Eighteenth.[8] Well, nobody knew what to do with these women. Then somebody thought of the idea of adjourning. When a meeting ain't running right, why, the thing to do is to adjourn, reorganize, and meet some time when the ones that are against you don't know when you are going to meet.

You know women are getting into more things that are embarrassing to men. You see, the first idea of giving them the vote was just to use the vote. But the women, contrary like they are, they wasn't satisfied with that. They started to take this equality thing serious. They begin to think they really was somebody. The women figured, "While we may not be as good as a man, we are at least as good as a politician." So the Scamps commenced to want to get in on the loot. As soon as they found out a political job took no experience to hold, that it only took experience to get, why they commenced to making themselves rather embarrassing around the Political Employment Bureau, and now every one of them calls themselves as a Number 2 Company of Mabel W. Willebrandt.[9] It was all right with the men when the women took the little committee assignments where there was no salary connected, but when they started to want to put their powdered nose into the feed trough, why, that brought on complications. Now they are wondering, "Was the Women's vote worth what they are asking for it?"

It's not only that way with Tammany Hall, but it's getting that way all over. Women that used to wouldn't think of gossiping anywhere but over a back fence, now won't say a word about you till the meeting has been duly called to order. It's scattered scandal around more. It's brought it more into the open. It's changed lots of things around. Families that used to didn't know there was a Restaurant in town are looking over the menu cards on days when the Ladies Auxiliary of the "Pork Barrel Political Society" is in session.

To us fellows that are not in Politics, we are tickled to death to see the Women folks dealing such misery to the Politicians. And in the long run it's good for humanity. Every job a Woman can grab off, it just drives another Politician to either work or the poor house.

And you know this next Congress that meets now pretty soon. Did you just notice the amount of Crepe De Chine and Lingerie there was mixed up in it? Why pretty near every prominent man we ever had in Politics has got a Daughter entered in that Congress. 'Course that's another trouble with Politics, it breeds Politics. So that makes it pretty hard to stamp out. The only way to do it is at the source. We got to get Birth Control among Politicians. We have to do that in order that they don't bring more Politicians into the World.

—April 23, 1928

[T]his Nineteenth Amendment is worrying more people in the Country than the Eighteenth. It's not only caused millions of men to go hungry, (by their wives being away at a rally) but it is causing a lot of them to go jobless, all because the whole thing was a misunderstanding. The men give 'em the vote, and never meant for them to take it seriously. But being Women they took the wrong meaning and did.

—April 23, 1928

LONDON: Another American woman just now swam in from France. Her Husband was carried from the boat suffering from cold and exposure. She has two children; the smallest a girl is swimming over tomorrow.

Yours for a revised edition of the Dictionary explaining which is the weaker sex.

—August 28, 1926

Funny thing about that White House: It wears down the most hardy of our men folks, but the women seem to thrive on it.

—October 11, 1934

The League of Women Voters are here in the convention demanding these planks in the next platform: Democratic women want birth control for Republicans, and Republican women want equal corruption for both sexes.

—August 25, 1930

You see there is no stopping these Women when they get started. Why I wouldn't be a bit surprised that it won't be no time till some Woman will become so desperate politically and just lose all prospectus of right and wrong and maybe go from bad to worse and finally wind up in the Senate.

Now you know that no Father or Mother ever had any idea that the offspring would ever darken a Senate door. 'Course up to now there has been no need for anything resembling a Woman in the Senate, especially an Old Woman, for there is more old Women in there already than there is in the Old Ladies Home. But they been in there on a pension for years, and they are awful nice old fellows, they don't do any particular harm to anyone. 'Course they don't do any great good. But they about break even and if they was out maybe somebody worse would be in.

—April 23, 1928

Everybody is always asking if women voting has made any real change in our political system. It has. It has just doubled the amount of candidates.

—October 11, 1931

The past week nine women in various parts of the U.S. shot and killed their husbands. In no line of our modern scientific advancement has progress been more marked than in the marksmanship of our weaker sex. It is true that woman is the weaker sex physically. But the automatic has proven to be the great stabilizer between the two sexes. Remington, and Smith and Wesson, have done more to advance the cause of woman's suffrage than all the arguments of its millions of believers.

—January 20, 1924

A wife is the cheapest thing you can get in the long run in the female line. Why, if ninety percent of the wives of this country ever got an allowance of $1,500 in their lifetime, they would have their husbands examined by a lunacy commission.

—June 3, 1923

There was a woman convicted here in New York last week for killing a man. These women will learn after a while that you can't go out and kill a man you are not married to and get away with it.

If you see some man you want to shoot, why, marry him first. The law only protects a man as far as the altar. Then it is every devil for himself.

—March 25, 1923

If women insist on having men's privileges, they have to take men's chances.

—November 1, 1925

What's holding women back nowadays is they stop to powder their noses. I tell you, when you take time out for powdering, a day is just about gone....Why you want your nose, which has a natural tendency to be red, to be changed to white, while your cheeks, which are naturally white, to be red, I also don't know.

—September 7, 1924

WHAT'S THIS GENERATION COMING TO? I BET YOU THE TIME **ain't** FAR OFF WHEN A WOMAN WON'T KNOW **any more** THAN A MAN.

—April 29, 1923

They keep telling American women that they should have equality—real equality with men, like they do in Russia. Well, the difference as I could see in Russia in equality was—the women had a pick and shovel over there. The men didn't.

All along the trans-Siberian Railway, the women would be harvesting the crops, the men would come down to watch the train come in.

—October 14, 1934

Although the gamest women can keep back tears in sorrow, they can't keep them back in happiness.

—July 27, 1924

I'M SO GLAD YOU LADIES LENGTHENED YOUR DRESSES...**concealment** HAS LED MORE MEN TO THE ALTAR THAN EXPOSURE HAS.

—Notes

There are two types of men in the world that I feel sincerely sorry for. One is the one that is always saying "I know the Mississippi River," and the other is the one is the fellow that thinks he "knows women."

—June 9, 1927

Headline says "Society Women of New York Smoking Pipes." The only way to break 'em from it is not watch 'em do it.

—April 8, 1932

Every sensational case nowadays has its mother-in-law. If these mothers protected their daughters as much before they get into court as they do after they get in there, they wouldn't get into court. Too bad they don't fight for their daughter's reputation as quick as they will for their daughter's alimony.

—January 26, 1927

Women love to say that they don't want war, and that they have to bear the brunt of it, which, of course, they really do, but if you ever noticed, all their speeches and denunciations of war is after it's over, they never do it in the making of one. Six or eight women could prevent war. The wives of the Prime Ministers, Diplomats, and Presidents, would only have to say, "If you allow war to come to this country, I will leave you, so help me."

But history...[has] no record of one having been left for that reason, though left for everything else. But when he comes home some day and says, "Honey, I guess you saw the extras on the street, I had to declare war." She says, "I know it, darling, and we will lick the very pants of the other old, mean nation."

—December 17, 1933

The permanent wife is the one without advice.

—January 26, 1927

Women promised us that if they had the vote they would clean up politics. They did! They got in and cleaned up more than the men did.

—June 2, 1935

MONEY AND WOMEN ARE THE MOST **sought** AFTER AND LEAST **understood** OF ANY TWO THINGS WE HAVE.

—June 2, 1935

You know, many a man has got a licking, because his wife has said, "Go on! Get, John, you ain't a-going to let him say that are you." Women are not the weak, frail, little flowers that they are advertised. There has never been anything invented yet, including war, that a man would enter into, that a woman wouldn't too.

—December 17, 1933

[A]ll the wars in the world, even if you won 'em, can't repay one mother for the loss of one son. But even at that, when she says to you "That's my oldest boy's picture, he was lost in the war," there is behind that mist in her eyes a shine of pride.

—December 17, 1933

Russia is putting five million women under arms for the next war. Well, we got five million that would do it. There is at least that many here who have tried everything else that men do with the exception of shouldering a musket.

—March 28, 1930

WILL ROGERS WAS A LIFELONG PROPONENT of a consumption tax
in lieu of an income tax:

"So why don't they use a national sales tax? That is the only fair
and just tax. Have no tax on necessary food and moderately priced
clothes, but put a tax on every other thing you buy or use. Then
the rich fellow who buys more and uses more, has no way of getting
out of his paying his share."

A fiscal conservative, he also wanted national debt reduced
before taxes were lowered.

"When is the time to pay off a debt if it's not when you are
doing well? All government statistics say that seventy percent of
every dollar paid in the way of taxes goes to just keeping up on
the interest and a little dab of amortization of our national debts.

In other words, if we didn't owe anything our taxes would be only less than one-third what they are today. Now, here is what I can't savvy. Why is it that one of us, in fact all of us, will work and save, and stint all of our lives? For what? Why, to leave something to our children. Now that is what we will do as individuals, but, when it comes to collectively, why it looks like we will break our necks to see how much we can leave them owing."

You have office holders to pass bills about taxes and what is the money from taxes for, anyhow? Why, it's to pay the office holders that passed the tax bills in the first place.

—Notes

We don't seem to be able to even check crime, so why not legalize it and put a heavy tax on it? Make the tax for robbery so high that a bandit couldn't afford to rob anyone unless they knew they had a lot of dough.

We have taxed other industries out of business; it might work here.

—March 20, 1931

Interest on the Federal Debt is sky high and we owe billions. That's where all the money goes we pay in taxes; most of it goes to pay Interest on money we owe.

Let's sell off enough of this country to somebody and pay off all National Debts, then the taxes wouldn't be nearly as much. The Democrats will agree to peddle Texas and Florida. And I am certain the Republicans will let Massachusetts and Rhode Island go.

—December 16, 1928

I see a good deal of talk from Washington about lowering taxes. I hope they do get 'em lowered down enough so people can afford to pay 'em.

—December 28, 1924

IF YOU MAKE ANY MONEY, THE GOVERNMENT **shoves** YOU IN THE CREEK ONCE A YEAR WITH IT IN YOUR POCKETS, AND ALL THAT DON'T GET **wet** YOU CAN KEEP.

—January 28, 1934

New York City laid off 600 cops. They claim they have no tax money. No wonder! All their influential men are engaged in tax-exempt occupations. What they got to do is tax crime. Put such a stiff tax on it that only high-class gangsters can afford it. It's the riff-raff that makes any business disreputable.

—Recording

Well, I haven't had much time lately to dope out new jokes. I have been helping the girls in the *Follies* make out their income tax. I was able to help on account of my equal knowledge of making out income tax with any man in the world, as none of us know a thing about it.

Look what I saved them on bathing suits! And I defy even a Congressional investigating Committee…to say that a bathing suit on a beautiful girl don't come under the heading of legitimate advertising.

—April 8, 1923

The lower tax issue was dragged out and dusted off. When a Party can't think of anything else, they always fall back on lower taxes. It has a magic sound to a voter, just like fairyland is spoken of…by all children. But no child has ever seen it, neither has any voter lived to see when his taxes were lowered.

—October 19, 1924

Put big taxes on everything of a luxury nature. You do that and let the working man know the rich have paid before they got it and you will do more than any one thing to settle some of the unrest and dissatisfaction that you hear every day....No Slick lawyer...can get you out of a sales tax....The poor fellow [will] know you are paying for it and he will not feel envious of you. He will even encourage you to buy more so it will help out the government.

—November 2, 1924

Monte Carlo has the right idea. Fix a game so you are going to get people's money, but the people don't know you are getting it. A fellow can always get over losing money in a game of chance, but he...can never get over money thrown away to a government in taxes.

—August 28, 1926

Our Secretary of the Treasury is today's headliner, borrowing one billion, one hundred million at three percent. Could have gotten it at about one-and-a-half [percent], but wanted to give the boys a break. This means they are going to finance by borrowing instead of increasing taxes on those able to pay.

It is too close to election [time] to antagonize the big boys.

—August 31, 1931

> ## IT AIN'T **taxes** THAT IS HURTING THE COUNTRY, IT'S **interest**. THIS COUNTRY RIGHT NOW IS OPERATING ON A DOLLAR DOWN, AND A DOLLAR A WEEK.
>
> —January 6, 1934

Say, did you see a few days ago the papers where a burglar sent in his income tax? He apologized for not doing better on his hauls. He said he hadn't done so well this year. That was on account of [it being] an election year. Competition is too keen.

—March 9, 1924

If I was running for President, I certainly wouldn't pull that old tax saving gag. I would just announce, "Folks, I don't believe I will be able to save you anything. Taxes are going to be high, and the only thing I would advise you to do, is not have anything—they will tax it away from you."

—October 19, 1924

You know, people don't want their taxes lowered near as much as the politicians try to make you believe. People want *just* taxes more than they want *lower* taxes.

—November 2, 1924

There should be tax on every man that wanted to get a government appointment, or be elected to office. In two years that tax alone would pay our national debt.

—March 22, 1925

There is one scheme that Congress could come forward with that would raise [a lot of] money.…[t]hat would be putting a tax on murders, robberies, and liquors. But I don't think they would do that. You can't, in politics, go against your constituency.

—August 28, 1926

About the only way…it would be fair to everybody, would be for Congress to go into secret session, allow no telephones…no visitors, so no outside lobbyists can get 'em, then tax everything they want to tax, then announce, "Boys, it's all over, there is no use shooting at us now."

As it is now, we are taxing everybody without a lobby.

—February 29, 1935

The Supreme Court ruled that a bootlegger had to pay income tax. We ought to have our national debt paid in a couple of years now.

—May 17, 1927

THE CRIME OF TAXATION IS NOT IN THE **taking** OF IT; IT'S IN THE WAY IT'S **spent**.

—March 20, 1932

Every time Congress starts to tax some particular industry, it rushes down with its main men and they scare [Congress] out of it. Now they got such a high inheritance tax...that you won't catch those old rich boys dying promiscuously like they did. This [law] makes patriots out of everybody. You sure do die for your country if you die from now on.

—March 23, 1932

You can't legitimately kick on taxes when the money has been made; it's taxes on farms, ranches, and business property that have lost money for years that folks have a holler coming.

—August 3, 1933

Now if a tax on gasoline keeps up all the roads, why wouldn't a tax on light wines and beer keep up the House of Representatives; one on Coca Cola and Jamaica ginger and Camembert cheese keep up the Senate; White Rock and cracked ice the state legislatures, and so forth.

And make each stay within the budget. For instance, if people wasn't drinking much beer we wouldn't have [as] many congressmen; if toothpaste and facial creams has a slump, cut the President's salary in proportion.

—January 5, 1932

[Income tax has] made more liars out of the American people than golf.

—March 15, 1929

The Secretary of the Treasury come out with a plan to put a bigger and better tax on these big estates—a tremendous big inheritance tax, is what it is. This is, men who died and on an estate of say, ten million dollars, the government would take about ninety percent and then give the offspring ten.

Then on an estate of one hundred and two hundred million the government just takes all of that and notifies the heirs: Your father died a pauper here today and he is being buried by the MEBA, that's the Millionaires' Emergency Burial Association.

—April 28, 1935

I think it is a good law [inheritance tax] to turn your assets over to the government—'course they can do some darn fool things with it, no telling what, maybe some things as foolish as the heirs of the deceased.

—May 13, 1934

We will never get anywhere with our finances till we pass a law saying that every time we appropriate something, we got to pass another bill along with it, stating where the money is coming from.

—February 12, 1932

The papers headline it any time somebody gets a refund on their income tax....It's news if you can get anything out of the government, but if the government gets anything out of you, that ain't news, that's just a habit.

—March 30, 1933

You read editorials that say it is a shame that these rich men get out of all that income tax, and us poor fellows have to pay. Well, we pay it, but brother, we try just as hard to get out of it as he did. Boy, we go out and get experts and lawyers and everything else to come in, and any guy that don't do that is a half-wit.

—June 4, 1933

What would be the matter with using every cent [from a liquor tax] for charity and unemployment relief? And make the tax very high, even as high as fifty percent. If it was a fifty percent tax, and it went to charity, you couldn't drink alone. Some poor family would be drinking with you. You get a beer; somebody gets a loaf of bread. Anybody give a big champagne party and spend hundreds of dollars, not even a communist could kick on it for the needy get half of it.

—July 20, 1933

> I SEE NOW WHAT MAKES A CONGRESSMAN SO **unpopular**. HE JUST WILL NOT FIX A TAX THAT **falls** ON NOBODY.
>
> —August 4, 1933

The way they got it now, when you get all through with your taxes, you add an extra ten percent, that's the "cover charge."

—April 13, 1934

Boy, when you bring us down to taxes, you're going to hear a howl like a pet coon. You know this money the government is throwing away—well, where's it coming from? Everybody says, "Where's the money coming from we're spending?" Well, I don't know, but just offhand, I'd say it's coming from those that got it, you know. Now I don't know. That may be just a rough idea of mine. I don't know, but I kinda believe that's where it's coming from.

There's one good thing about the American form of government. The fellow that's got nothing, he don't pay nothing. You know.

But the big yell comes nowadays from, the big taxpayers. I bet you when the Pilgrims landed at Plymouth Rock and they had the whole of the American continent for themselves—you know, just the Pilgrims who landed up there, and all they had to do to get an extra hundred and sixty acres was shoot another Indian. Well, I bet you anything they kicked on the price of ammunition. I bet they said, "What's this country coming to?" You know, what I mean—like we're doing now. "What's this country coming to? We have to spend a nickel for powder."

I don't know, ain't it funny? No matter what we pay—whether we pay high taxes, low taxes, medium taxes, the yell is always the same, a hundred percent. Of course, we know our government is costing us more than it's worth, but do you know of any other, cheaper government that's running around? Do you? I mean, if you do, they'll sell you a ticket there anytime.

Now you can try Russia. I was over there. Yeah, you can try Russia. There's no income tax in Russia, but there's no income.

Now Hitler—Hitler ain't got no sales tax—you know what I mean—but he ain't selling anything. Well, that's fine. Mussolini, you don't have to pay a poll tax to vote in Italy, you know, but nobody votes.

So the whole question is, "How can we make such a holler on what the government wants to collect back from us?" Oh, I don't know anymore about this thing than an economist does, and God knows, he don't know anything.

—Good Gulf Show, April 1935

EDUCATION

WILL ROGERS WAS A PEACEFUL MAN. He avoided conflicts and confrontations. He was a Westerner who did not sport a handgun or collect rifles. He did not hunt. This lack of interest in weapons might have been his nature, or it might have been due to the memory of a teen-age lesson that left more than a casual impression.

Attending the Kemper Military Academy in Boonville, Missouri, seventeen-year-old Will Rogers was forced to drill, learning the Manual-of-Arms. For hours the cadets would march up and down the parade ground, following the commands of their instructors, handling their rifles in every prescribed way. These military exercises were intended to teach raw recruits the precise motions of loading and carrying their rifles. Rogers became proficient at drilling and he knew that the maneuvers were impressive to civilian spectators.

Back at home, he wanted to show some friends what he had learned. Dressed in his smart cadet uniform, he borrowed a cowhand's rifle and shouting the instructor's usual commands to himself, he went through the entire exercise, ending with the slamming of the rifle butt onto the ground. While the rifles at the Academy were always unloaded, the cowhand's gun contained live ammunition. The hard slam on the ground caused the gun to fire.

The bullet shot straight upwards, grazing Rogers's forehead and leaving a life-long scar. He later described his two years at Kemper Military Academy in this way: "I spent one year in the Fourth Grade and the other in the Guard House; one was as bad as the other." One dark night, he left the Academy and ended his formal education.

———————

Does College pay? It does if you are a good open field runner!

—Notes, 1926

That education is sorter like a growing town. They get all excited when they start to get an increase, and they set a civic Slogan of "Fifty Thousand by the end of next year." Well that's the Guy that sets a College education as his Goal. When they get the fifty thousand they want to go on to make it a Hundred, and the Ambitious College graduate wants to go on and make it a Post graduate...[of course] when [the town] get to a half million New York will be twenty million, so they are no higher in the ladder comparatively than they were.

And the Education Guy, he is the same. He finds he gets his post-graduate course that all the other Professors have one too, and lots of 'em a half-dozen.

—July 5, 1931

Is education necessary to football? No! A good coach and good interference is all that's necessary.

—Notes, 1926

This College Spirit thing is kinder overestimated. Men will do things every day for money that all the spirit in the world you try to assemble can't make 'em do.

—December 6, 1925

[Imagine,] they call Domestic Science a course now. In the old days you learned that at home. You had to be good at it for you had to eat it.

—Notes

When do you think a College athlete should turn pro? Not till he has earned all he can at College as an amateur.

—Notes, 1926

Do you think our Colleges are becoming commercialized? No, no more than the Steel Industry.

—Notes, 1926

Say, there is an awful lot in the papers the last few days about experiments these College professors are making with rats. One professor wanted to find out what effect athletics had on a rat's intelligence. He wanted to see if it was dumber, or keener after running back punts and tackling another rat for a while.

The experiment showed that the rat was keener with athletics by him, demanding free tuition and board and ten percent of the gate on all big games. The rat with no exercise wound up as a bond salesman.

—September 27, 1929

We have to keep our schools going. There is nothing else that teachers can do.

—Notes

AMERICA IS BECOMING SO EDUCATED THAT **ignorance** WILL BE A NOVELTY. I WILL **belong** TO A SELECT FEW.

—Notes

It's better to turn out a good football coach than ten College presidents.

—Notes, 1926

The only salvation I can see for the young nowadays is to increase the college term to an additional four years....You say: "Well, what could they learn in another four years?" Well, there must be some little something about making a living that they haven't learned yet. They could kind of work on that for the next four years.

—June 2, 1935

It's the contacts that you make at colleges that keep you selling bonds all your life.

— *"How to be Funny"*

And your fraternity? That can get you a lot of drinks in strange places, for generally the bartender is another fraternity brother.

— *"How to be Funny"*

No sir, they can all knock education that want, but it's the college men that carry on, and fill the jobs, and work for the ignorant men that own the business.

— *"How to be Funny"*

Why don't they pass a Constitutional Amendment prohibiting anybody learning anything? And if it works as good as the Prohibition one did, in five years we would have the smartest race of people on Earth.

—January 4, 1925

I have a lot of big ideas. They just don't seem to work out. There must be a bit of college professor in me somewhere.

—August 31, 1930

In the old days, boys wanted an education. They even had reading, writing, and arithmetic, instead of football. Up to then boys had gone there for their heads and not for their shoulders.

—August 26, 1928

Harvard is the home of culture and poor football. Everybody in Harvard can speak good English but almost nobody can make a touchdown.

—Notes, 1926

Today it's open field running that gets your old College somewhere and not a pack of spectacled orators or a mess of Civil Engineers.

—Notes, 1926

Nicholas Murray Butler[10] deserves a lot of credit. He has taken a College right in the heart of New York City, a place where you would think would be the very last place to get anybody interested in education and he has built it up just by making rich men think that by leaving something to the school it would help the rest of America forget how some of them got the money.

—April 24, 1927

Harvard's English Department is becoming discouraged. Our English is getting worse than our habits.

—July 24, 1928

THERE IS **nothing** AS STUPID AS AN EDUCATED MAN IF YOU GET HIM OFF THE THING HE WAS **educated** IN.

—July 5, 1931

I was just a-thinking what I would have to do if I was to start out to help out my old school. "Drumgoole" was a little one-room log cabin four miles east of Chelsea, Indian Territory.

It was all Indian kids went there, and I, being part Cherokee, had enough white in me to make my honesty questionable.

—September 29, 1929

It seems a scientist is a man that can find out anything and nobody in the world has any way of proving whether he really found out anything, or not.

—January 13, 1929

Somebody just left Yale University eight million dollars as an endowment to study humans, including senior classmen. They want to figure out why Notre Dame can throw a forward pass further than a green apple.

A College president's work nowadays consists of thinking up new things for the students to play with that looks like studying.

All this stuff would have been a kick to Abe Lincoln, wouldn't it?

—February 15, 1929

I tell you if every book on old things was thrown in the river, and everybody had nothing to study but the future, we would be about 200 years ahead of what we are.

—January 13, 1929

Chicago University come out yesterday with a terrible radical idea. They proposed to graduate a student as soon as he knows enough.

That shows you that higher education is making progress. It's taken two thousand years to think of such a thing. Heretofore they have made the smart ones stay there for four years, just to keep the dumb ones company.

—November 20, 1930

The football season is closing and college life is about over for the year.

—November 25, 1928

> THE COLLEGE PRESIDENT WILL BE **looking** OVER THE GATE RECEIPTS TO SEE IF HE **stays** ANOTHER YEAR.
>
> —November 25, 1928

Say, any of you that have kids in schools, either grammar, high, or College, it don't make any difference, but can any of you parents get head or tail of what they are doing? What they are taking? What they are learning?

All the kids I know, either mine or anybody's, none of 'em can write so you can read it, none of 'em can spell, figure, or tell you even what bounds Korea.

—July 31, 1932

In school, if you tell where a Latin word was originally located, and how it's been manhandled and orphanized down to the present day, they will claim that you have the nucleus of a "thesis" and you are liable to get a horde of "credits."

'Course you can't go out and get a job on it, but these old professors value it mighty highly. And us old dumb parents, we just string along and do the best we can, and send 'em as long as we are able, because we want them to have the same handicaps the others have.

—July 31, 1932

The papers today say that illiteracy has decreased. The more that learn how to read, the less learn how to make a living. That's one thing about a little education, it spoils you for actual work. The more you know, the more you think somebody owes you a living.

—September 4, 1931

Education is just like everything else. You got to judge it by results. Here we are better educated—according to educational methods—than we ever were. It's costing us more than it's worth, yet the smarter the nation gets, the more wars it has. The dumb ones are too smart to fight.

Trying to live *past* our parents and not *up to* 'em is one of our drawbacks.

—July 31, 1932

Now here is a nice letter from a college President. He wanted to give me a degree, said they had given the Cabinet, the Supreme Court, and leading Industrialists degrees, and had been hooded and gowned. I have this same play come up a time or two and I think these guys are kidding. If they are not, they ought to be.

Degrees have lost prestige enough as it is, without handing 'em around to second-hand comedians, and it's this handing 'em out too promiscuously that has helped to cheapen 'em. Let a guy get in there and battle four years if he wants one, and don't give him one just because he happens to hold a good job in Washington, or manufactures more monkey wrenches than anybody else, or because he might be fool enough to make people laugh. Keep 'em just for those kids that have worked hard for 'em. Keep 'em believing in 'em. They are stepping out in the world with nothing but that sheet of paper. That's all they got; our civilization don't offer 'em anything else. We offer him nothing. He steps into a world not of his making, so let's at least don't belittle his badge.

—May 10, 1935

It's funny how quick a college boy can find out that the world is [all] wrong. He might go out in the world from High School and live in it, and make a living in it for years and think it wasn't such a bad place. But, let him go to College and he will be the first one down on the Square on May Day to shout "Down with the Government."

—March 29, 1931

It's no trouble to tell the successful educational institution these days. It's the one that can afford a new stadium next year.

—November 25, 1928

None of these big professors will come out and tell you what our education might be lacking. They know as it is now it's a racket, and you couldn't get me to admit that making movies was bunk, either. None of us will talk against our own graft.

—July 31, 1932

Did you ever see or hear of a thing so nutty in your life as…the chain letters that are sweeping the country: Imagine, everybody was to send a dime and everybody was to receive sixteen hundred dollars.

I tell you, when a country falls for a thing like that, it just makes you doubly sure that our school system is a failure.

—May 5, 1935

THE ARMED FORCES

WILL ROGERS FAVORED A STRONG MILITARY as the best way to deter an attack on America, but he was strongly opposed to the streak of foreign adventurism that ran through American foreign policy starting with the Spanish-American War. His ideal was to have a strong military but to keep it at home, and not to interfere in the various revolutions and upheavals that plagued the world, particularly Latin America. The introduction of U.S. Marines into many different countries was a constant source of material for his *Ziegfeld Follies* performance and his syndicated columns.

Rogers was particularly concerned about the dismal state of American military aviation. A trip to Europe in the mid-1920s only reinforced his concern as he saw the advanced state of development of European military air power. Although he thought war was a terrible waste of human life, he did not have the starry-eyed expectation that the world could negotiate war out of existence. The various disarmament initiatives of the 1920s caused Rogers great concern lest America leave itself defenseless in the face of potential aggressors.

Rogers also had great concern for the plight of veterans. The unwillingness of the government in Washington to do right by the veterans of the "Great War" (World War I) was a continuing national shame, and Rogers returned to this theme from time to time.

This must be American territory, I don't see any Marines.

—April 19, 1931

Well, they brought our soldiers back from Germany last week. Would have brought them back sooner, but we didn't have anybody in Washington who know where they were. Had to leave them over there anyway; two of them hadn't married yet.

—February 18, 1923

Pacifists say that if you are ready for war, you will have one. I bet you there has not been a man insulting Jack Dempsey since he has become heavyweight champion.

—August 10, 1924

You can't pick up a paper without reading where our Marines have landed to keep some nation from shooting each other, and if necessary we shoot them to keep them from shooting each other.

—July 5, 1925

A mythical drama in an investigating committee room in Washington, D.C.:

CHAIRMAN: General Billy Mitchell, do you think we are prepared to go to war with our present airships?

MITCHELL: Yes, Mr. Chairman, I think we could if we used good judgment in picking our enemy. I think we have an even chance with Monaco.

CHAIRMAN: Then you mean to insinuate that we couldn't whip Japan in the air? Then tell me, how long do think it would take Japan to take Honolulu by air?

MITCHELL: I don't know the mileage so I don't know how long it would take 'em to get there.

—March 1, 1925

Our Army and Navy have degenerated so since the last war, a lot of governors are ashamed to have a parade and show how little they have got. We are the only nation in the world that waits till we get into a war before we start getting ready for it.

—August 10, 1934

[LETTER TO SENATOR BORAH:] I want to tell you, war is a business with some of these [countries]. When a war shows up they don't have to stop and put in a draft and sing songs and make three-minute speeches and appoint dollar-a-year men. All that has been attended to long before the war ever broke out. All their soldiers are trained between wars—not after one starts. You see, we have been lucky that way, all of our wars have waited on us till we could get ready. But one day we may have one where the enemy won't wait.

You think I'm kidding? Well, you are just another Senator, if you do!

—March 12, 1932

Now this is what I am trying to get you to understand, Calvin. These guys over here in Europe, no matter how little or big the country, they have left the ground and are in the air. Nobody is walking but us; everybody else is flying. So in a few years, when somebody starts dropping something on us, don't say I didn't warn you.

—October 23, 1926

My advice to Mr. Coolidge on preparedness is slowly bearing fruit. Here are his exact words in a speech Saturday: "What we need, and all that we need for national protection, is adequate protection." You couldn't ask for a clearer statement than that. What a hungry man needs, and all that he needs... is adequate food....

—January 30, 1927

I TELL YOU, ANY EXPERIMENT THAT IS BEING **made** IN THE AIR, IS NOT A WASTE OF TIME OR MONEY. OUR DEFENSE, OFFENSE, AND ALL HAVE GOT TO **come** FROM THE AIR.

—May 29, 1932

We better start doing something about our defense. Build all we can, and then take care of nothing but our own business, and we will never have to use it. If something happened to us right now, and it comes to a showdown, the shape we are in with our Army,

Navy, and Aviation, there would be such a howl, Coolidge would have a tough time not being impeached.

All I got to go by is history, and history don't record that "Economy" ever won a war. So I believe I would save money somewheres else, even if I had to work a little shorter handed around the Capitol there.

—January 16, 1927

When we nearly lose the next war, as we probably will, we can lay it onto one thing and that will be jealousy of the army and navy toward aviation. They have belittled it ever since it started and will keep on doing it until they have something dropped on them from one, and even then they will say it wasn't a success.

—March 11, 1927

Been visiting and listening to speeches in both ends of the Capitol all day, debating on a big Navy bill. Was talking to a lady Congressman and she said to me, "Why do all those men say that a big navy will bring peace?" I told her, "Well, even if it don't bring peace, it will come in mighty handy."

—January 30, 1934

Say, did you know that one time we had our troops occupying part of Siberia?...We would send soldiers anywhere that could get ten signers to a petition that said they wanted us. We was in the humanity business and we was going to do it right.

—September 26, 1932

Spain discovered half the world, her ships were on every sea, but she let her navy run down and wound up in the class Z league. Look at Holland, great country, big as England...but did you ever hear of them when they talk of what the big powers want? No, you would think they were Rhode Island. Why? No Navy. Brazil is bigger than England, France, Italy, and Japan and has more natural resources than all of them combined. Yet she couldn't get a Chamber of Commerce Membership rally. Same old answer: no Navy.

—March 16, 1930

[There's] one thing these old boys with a big navy are scared of and that's submarines. They are always claiming they are inhuman, and not a civilized mode of warfare.

It would be rather interesting to see published the names of the weapons that are considered a pleasure to be shot by.

—April 30, 1935

[The House] pass[ed] a bonus bill [for World War I veterans].

All the soldier has to do to get a bonus now is to die. Those that they don't get to die for nothing they are offering an inducement to die now for somewhere in the neighborhood of five hundred dollars.

If your bonus comes to less than fifty dollars, why they are going to pay that to you. They ain't going to ask you to die for fifty dollars. No, sixty is about the lowest.

—April 6, 1924

HARBIN, MANCHURIA: Say if I didn't run into another batch of Marines here! Marines are not soldiers, they are tourists. I find 'em all over.

—March 19, 1932

Well, lots of war news in the papers today. I knew it was coming when I saw that we had cut down on our Army and Navy.

If you want to know when a war is coming, just watch the U.S....and see when it starts cutting down on its defense. It's the surest barometer in the world.

—May 16, 1933

If you haven't bought a poppy this morning as you read this, go right now and do so. The soldier boys in the hospitals make 'em and it's for a great charity. The further we get in years away from war, the less we think of it; but it's not these fellows' fault. They never thought much of it even at the time.

—May 25, 1934

I hope you noticed that we now have the Marines all back in America. It's the first time in years. Some of the boys like it here— they think it is a great country and a lot of them are going to take out citizenship papers.

—January 27, 1935

CRIME AND LAW

ROGERS HAD THE PERSPECTIVE of a small town resident when considering crime and the criminal justice system, particularly as practiced in big cities. He had little sympathy for "sophisticated" defenses, such as insanity, and utter contempt for the widespread practice of granting bail, pardons, and paroles.

He harkened back to a simpler time, when murderers were locked up before trial, promptly tried, and then hung.

Although he was from the West, he did not argue that the solution was a well-armed citizenry; he considered that a recipe for civil war. He abhorred the availability of automatic weapons. Rather he favored simple, straightforward police work by honest policemen, with no favoritism for the wealthy or powerful.

And, of course, he was amused by the absurdity of Prohibition, with everyone, in all walks of life openly and notoriously violating not only the law, but the Constitution, while paying public lip service to the importance of supporting temperance for the country's moral benefit.

———————

You haven't seen a Policeman walking on the Sidewalk since Henry Ford perfected his first Carburetor.

—May 31, 1925

We don't give our criminals much punishment, but we sure give 'em plenty of publicity.

—February 2, 1934

That automatic pistol, it's all right to have it invented, but it should never have been allowed outside the army, and then only in wartime.

—September 20, 1925

Today, addle-brains can go and buy a gun any place they want to.

—September 20, 1925

'Course the way we do things, always have done things, and always will do things, there just has to be so much graft. We wouldn't feel good if there wasn't.

—November 25, 1934

Supply and Demand regulates robberies the same as it regulates everything else. The supply of people who have money to be robbed of will never exceed the demand to rob them. In other words, as soon as there is a man that has a dollar, there is a robber to take it.

—August 28, 1926

HEADLINES IN ALL THE PAPERS SAY: "Authorities Having Trouble Rounding Up Twelve Escaped Lunatics.'"

The main trouble is recognizing 'em. I bet they get a different twelve back in.

—June 5, 1930

Nowadays it's about as big a crime to be dumb, as it is to be dishonest.

—February 3, 1929

The automatic pistol is much more dangerous and destructive than the old six-shooter, as poison gas is over perfume.

—September 20, 1925

In this drug dealer's case in New York, do you know what will happen when the whole thing goes through the courts? Why, the truck drivers will be sent to jail and the leaders will open bigger and better than ever.

—October 17, 1929

None of the habeas corpusing and suspended sentences or appealing it when you commit a crime over here in England. You just wake up surrounded by a small space.

Some delegation ought to come over here and study British justice.

—January 24, 1930

If there is one thing that it would be laughable for this country to try and show the rest of the world how to do, it would be run a court.

Of all the cockeyed things we have in this country at the present time, it's some of the judges and courts and justices. Why, we got more bandits out on bail than we got people for 'em to rob.

—December 18, 1930

The future of bank robberies is to arrange some way to charge admission. So many people seeing robberies for free is what's killing the business.

—June 20, 1934

THE BOOZE SOME BOOTLEGGERS SOLD WAS SO strong THEY HAD TO dilute IT WITH ALCOHOL.

—Digest, 1919

There is a thousand policemen to see that you don't park your car too long, where there is not one to see that your child is not kidnapped. Every man on the street can have an automatic pistol in every pocket, yet he will never be searched. But you let your taillight be out, and you are in for life.

—May 31, 1925

We are a good-natured bunch of saps in this country. When a judge sentences a murderer, that's cruelty.

—June 30, 1930

Policemen used to carry a club that they used to crack over a crook's head. Now they have discarded that and they have a whistle. That's why there is so much crime. Whistling at a crook is not near as effective as to crack him on the bean with a hickory stick.

—May 31, 1925

Pardoning OF CONVICTS HAS BEEN ONE INDUSTRY THAT HASN'T BEEN HIT BY A **recession**.

—August 31, 1932

Some of our newspapers, if you take the murders out of them, would have nothing left but the title of the paper.

—September 20, 1925

American murder procedure is about as follows: foul enough to commit the crime, dumb enough to get caught, smart enough to prove you was crazy when you committed it, and fortunate enough to show you was too sane to hang.

—January 23, 1928

Our big problem is this discontent in our prisons. Hardly a day passes that prisoners don't show some little outward signs of uneasiness, such as shooting a few guards, burning some buildings, and giving a hint publicly that they want to participate in this era of prosperity through which we are struggling to make both ends meet.

It just looks like the boys in there don't appreciate how fortunate they are to have no installment payments to meet. I guess the next political campaign is liable to be based on "Bigger and Better Jails for Bigger and Better Prisoners!"

—August 7, 1929

Been reading in the papers today about the big crime combine that they said had been captured in the East. They had their own broadcasting station and they had enough guns that if they are not invited to the next disarmament conference, it will be on account of jealousy.

—October 17, 1929

Some new plan has got to be worked out in our prison system. Of course this may be a radical suggestion but couldn't they fix some way where the guards carried the guns, instead of the prisoners?

—December 12, 1929

I just give up reading murders. You no more than get a few details of one murder, than the afternoon papers bring you news of another.

The best-read man in the country couldn't tell you who killed who last week.

—June 18, 1934

I see where they convicted Al Capone[11] on five counts of silk underwear and four others. Now comes the "out on Bail, new Trial, Change of Venue, habeas corpus, stay of execution, and twenty-one other things" that the law invented to hinder justice.

—October 18, 1931

HERE IS A USUAL AP DISPATCH: "Four prisoners, three serving Life Terms, escaped from prison today!"

Nowadays the sentence reads: "You are sentenced to prison as long as it's made comfortable for you and you desire to remain. On checking out kindly let the warden know, so he will know how many there will be there for supper."

—April 13, 1934

Villains are getting as thick as college degrees, and sometimes on the same fellow.

—September 11, 1932

Americans are funny people; they never get het up over anything unless they are participating in it.

The fellow that ain't getting any corruption, he don't think that it can possibly be so common, or it would have reached him. And the ones that are getting some of it don't want it brought up.

—March 30, 1929

Let the government confiscate and forbid the entire sale of automatics, because they kill ten innocent people to one guilty one with those sprinkling guns, and then prohibit the six-shooters to anybody but police officers and when you catch a guy with a gun, send him to jail and don't just fine him!

—September 20, 1925

HEADLINE IN THE PAPERS SAYS: "Crooks from other cities are coming to Los Angeles."

The landlords here are going to have competition.

—Digest, 1920

It must be awfully monotonous belonging to some of these state parole boards. There is days and days when you just have to sit around, waiting for new criminals to be caught, so they can parole 'em.

—October 18, 1934

There must not be such a thing in this country as, what you would call an "amateur crook." Every person that is caught in some terrible crime, you find where he has been "paroled, pardoned, and pampered" by every jail, or insane asylum in the country.

—October 18, 1934

Crime today, say robbery, or some minor event, we fine them; and if it's confessed murder, why, they plead insanity. We go on the theory that if you confess you must be insane.

—August 28, 1925

Prohibition hasn't caused this wave of robberies. It's business depression. The poor robbers have to rob more people to make their quota than they used to. Give us good times again and the robber will get what he needs that day out of the first man robbed.

—December 1, 1930

If we are going to do away with capital punishment and sell guns to everybody, let's fix it so the party behind the gun will be at least a clear-headed marksman, instead of a drunken, drug-taking amateur. Think of the humiliation of being shot by one of the present-day gunmen.

—September 20, 1925

They are going to be more strict with these robbers. From now on, when they catch 'em, they are going to publish their names.

—Recording

> # I WOULD RATHER BE THE MAN WHO **bought** THE BROOKLYN BRIDGE THAN THE MAN WHO **sold** IT.
>
> —Notes

I see where the Mayor of New York City called a committee of one hundred to stop small graft. He said it had grown to such proportion that it was interfering with large graft, and that couldn't be allowed in New York.

—Notes

Lots of people think that racketeering and bootlegging and corruption are just a Fly-by-night business, run in a slipshod haphazard way. Well, you were never more wrong in your life. Why, meanness has always been better organized and conducted than righteousness.

—July 6, 1930

The New York Police Commissioner appointed a crime committee of twenty, to help him keep a list of crimes. If they hear of any crimes that he don't, then they report those crimes to him. Then at the end of the year, the one that has heard the most crimes gets a prize.

—May 16, 1929

The biggest question that is agitating the public is: Are all lunatics to be furnished with guns and ammunition? This gun thing is getting pretty serious here around New York. Everybody that hasn't got a gun is getting shot by somebody.

They pinch a thousand people a day for parking five minutes too long, but I have yet to read where a policeman ever searched a bunch of tough guys hanging around a place, to see if any of them carried concealed weapons. They could start searching everybody and in one day here in New York, they would get enough pistols to dam up the Hudson River.

—September 20, 1925

A Policeman used to have a Beat to Walk and he was watching out all the time for some crooked business. But nowadays if he saw a Robbery being committed he couldn't get out of the Traffic to get to it. The chances are he himself would be run over before he reached the sidewalk. So all they do nowadays is give you a Ticket.

—May 29, 1925

Do you know what has been the cause of the big increase in murders? It's been the manufacture of the automatic pistol. There is no skill or nerve required in using an automatic pistol. They should advertise those guns "Killing Made Easy! Just Hold the Trigger Down and We Guarantee You Somebody!"

And the more drunk or drugged a man is, the more he will hit.

—September 20, 1925

I see where a lot of men are advocating letting everybody carry guns with the idea that they will be able to protect themselves. In other words, just make civil war out of this crime wave.

—September 20, 1925

If you think that being armed protects you, why, how about the amount of policemen that are shot down here in New York? They are all armed.

—September 20, 1925

I interviewed Al Capone once, but I never did write the story. There was no way I could write it and not make a hero out of him.

What's the matter with us when our biggest gangster is our greatest national interest?

—Notes

In Sing Sing a few weeks ago, there were three young fellows electrocuted and there were over two thousand applications to the warden to see them go to their deaths. Imagine, if you can, people who want to see somebody else killed!

Anybody whose pleasure it is watching somebody else die, is about as little use to humanity as the person being electrocuted.

—June 7, 1925

Modern History has proven that there has never yet been a will left that was carried out exactly as the maker of the money intended. So if you are thinking of dying and have any money I would advise you to leave the following will: "Count up the Lawyers in the State and divide it among them."

—May 29, 1925

Police Chiefs had to organize to protect themselves against the keen competition of the Crooks. They worked out a way of sending fingerprints by Wireless and Radio. They seemed to think that was quite an achievement. They made no progress however in working out ways and means of capturing the person to be fingerprinted.

—May 29, 1925

Policemen are not Policemen any more they are just process servers. You shoot a man nowadays and they hand you a Ticket telling you to please appear in Court Monday at ten o'clock. If you can't come, send your Chauffeur.

—May 29, 1925

> ## CORRUPTION AND GOLF IS TWO THINGS THAT WE'D JUST AS WELL MAKE OUR MINDS UP TO **take up**, FOR THEY ARE BOTH GOING TO BE WITH US.
>
> —September 25, 1928

We just had the Police Chiefs from all over the World here last week. Most of them were robbed while here. So they really got to see crime at first hand.

—May 29, 1925

If it wasn't for Wills, lawyers would have to go to work at an essential employment.

—May 29, 1925

There is two types of Larceny—Petty and Grand—and the Courts will really give you a longer sentence for Petty than they do for Grand. They are supposed to be the same in the eyes of the law but Judges always put a little extra on you for Petty which is kind of a fine for stupidness: "If that's all you got you ought to go to jail longer."

There is only one way you can beat a Lawyer in a death case. That is to die with nothing. Then you can't get a Lawyer within ten miles of your house.

—May 29, 1925

In Memphis today, over twenty-five Policemen went to a hospital and volunteered to give blood transfusions to a kid that was near death.

I know that I am out of order in speaking about the good things that cops do, but I am one of the old-fashioned people who believe if someone pounces on me, I could holler for a policeman and he would come and help me out without me having to pay him anything.

—February 29, 1928

[T]he surest way out of this crime wave would be to punish the criminals, but of course, that is out of the question; that's barbarous and takes us back, as the hysterics say, to the days before civilization.

—September 20, 1925

Here, in New York nowadays, the so-called bad man is either an escaped lunatic, or a thick-headed drug user, or somebody full of terrible liquor. He shoots people just to get his picture in the papers.

—September 20, 1925

Everybody says for you to leave a will. Yes, leave a will so the Lawyers can misinterpret what you meant when you knew enough to know what you wanted to do with your money. To show you Justice there was forty-eight Lawyers on one side in this Jay Gould Will case.

—May 29, 1925

Racketeering is America's biggest industry.

—March 26, 1931

BUSINESS AND WALL STREET

NOVICE INVESTOR ROGERS DESCRIBED his personal experiences with the volatile New York Stock Market in the late 1920s and early 1930s. This is the report published in his syndicated column on November 10, 1929:

Now that Stock Market is all a puzzle to me. One time in New York last year when everybody was just raking in money with a shovel, so they all told me, well, I went to see Eddie Cantor, the actor. Now I had known and been a friend of Eddie's for many years and I was hearing that Eddie was piling up a fortune that Rockefeller couldn't vault over. So I go over to the New Amsterdam Theatre one night and call on Eddie.

Eddie thought I had come to persuade him to play a benefit, but I quietly whispered to him that I wanted him to make a few dollars without telling jokes for them, (or what went for jokes). But I told him I wanted to get in on this skinning of Wall Street. Everybody was doing it and I wanted to be in at the killing. I dident have anything particular against Wall Street, but knowing the geographical and physical attributes of the Street, I knew that it was crooked. (You can stand at the head of it, and you can only see to the bend. It just won't let you see all of it at once as short as it is.) I just said to myself I would like to be with the bunch that has the credit of straightening this Alley out.

Well Eddie had just that day made fifty thousand according to closing odds on the last commodity. I says show me the fifty. He then explained to me that he hadent the money, that that's what he could have made if he had sold. But he hadent sold, as tomorrow he should make at least another fifty, or only forty-nine.

Anyhow, he dident much want to take my money, knowing how hard I had worked for it, but I went on telling him I was forty-nine years [old] and had never in my life made a single dollar without having to chew some gum to get it. So he says, "Well I will buy you some of my bank stock. It's selling mighty high and with this little dab you got here you won't get much of it, but it's bound to go up, for banks make it whether the market goes up or down. Even if it stands still they are getting their interest while it's making up its mind what to do.

So he said I will get you some of this. Put it away and forget about it. Well I shook hands and told him that I had always known and said that he was the greatest Comedian on the stage but now I knew that he was the best financier we had in our profession. Well I went back to my own dressing room at my Theatre and I never was as funny in my life as I was that night. I had Wall Street by the tail.

I stayed up the next night till the papers come out to see what "our" Bank had closed at, and after reading it stayed up the rest of the night wondering if Eddie could possibly be wrong. Well one little drop brought on another. Each night I began to get unfunnier and unfunnier. This strain of being "In the Market" was telling on me. When there was a minus sign before my lone stock, I just was not unctuous. I dident want to tell Eddie. But finally I told him that on the morrow when the market opened, among those desiring to dispose, I would be among those present. I got out with a very moderate loss. Next day that bank stock went up big. But the whole thing is no place for a weak-hearted Comedian.

Wall Street had gone into one tailspin after another. You would pick up a paper in the morning and read the stock report and wouldent think there was that many "Minus Signs" in the world. If it kept on like that it would discourage gambling and that of course would be bad for the country. (That's what they said.)

—December 1, 1929

I have been trying my best to help Mr. Hoover and Wall Street "Restore Confidence." You take confidence, it's one of the hardest things in the world to get restored once it gets out of bounds.

—December 1, 1929

It's just as I have been constantly telling you: Don't gamble; take all your savings and buy some good stock, and hold it till it goes up, then sell it.

If it don't go up, don't buy it.

—October 31, 1929

Everybody likes to make a dollar his way but if he finds he is not allowed to make it his way, he is not going to overlook the chance of making it your way.

—December 5, 1933

Of course there was a lot of us dumb ones that couldn't understand it. We said, "Well if somebody lost money there, why, somebody else must have made it." You can't lose money to nobody, unless you drop it somewhere and nobody ever finds it.

—December 1, 1929

Everybody said it would have a demoralizing effect on the country for so many to have their paper profits rubbed out at once. That it would have the effect of making people more careful with their money, and thereby make it bad for speculation. That if people dident trade in stocks, why, Wall Street couldent exist.

So I says what can we do for 'em so they will keep on existing? Why, restore confidence! And that's what I have been doing for weeks. 'Course I haven't been buying anything myself. I wanted to give all the other folks a chance to have confidence first.

—December 1, 1929

If you think we are not prosperous and cuckoo both, read this: "Three Hundred Thousand Dollars for Seat on Stock Exchange!"

You pay that for a seat where nobody sits down. They stand and yell and sell something they haven't got and buy something they will never get. That's not a seat; that's a license to hold a sucker up when he buys and blackjack him when he sells—to commit petty larceny when he buys and grand larceny when he sells.

—November 24,.1927

Well all I know is just what I read in the Papers. Awful lot of news percolating here and there. This Stock Market thing has spoiled more appetites lately than bad cooking.

—November 10, 1929

I felt flattered when I saw that I was one to join in this great work of getting people back to contributing to Wall Street again. 'Course there is a lot of them that is going to take me time to get back. They not only lost confidence but they lost money.

—December 1, 1929

I am telling them that the country as a whole is "sound" and that it is bigger than Wall Street, and if they don't believe it, I show 'em the map.

December 1, 1929

America already holds the record for freak movements. Now we have a new one. It's called "restoring confidence." Rich men who never had a mission in life outside of watching a stock ticker are working day and night "restoring confidence."

Now I am not unpatriotic and I want to do my bit, so I hereby offer my services to my President, my country, and my friends around old Trinity Church, New York, to do anything that I can in this great movement. But you will have to give me some idea of where "confidence" is. And just who you want it restored to.

—November 19, 1929

You can't make a dollar without taking it from somebody.

—October 2, 1932

After all, everybody just can't live on gambling. Somebody has to do some work.

—November 24, 1929

There has never been a time in our history when as many fools are making money as now.

—June 11, 1929

EVERYBODY NOWADAYS IS SUGGESTING WAYS OF GETTING **prosperous** ON **somebody else's** MONEY.

—February 17, 1931

It's the greatest game I ever saw. It looks like you can't lose. Everybody buys to sell and nobody buys to keep. What's worrying me is who is going to be the last owner. It's just like an auction; the only one stuck is the last one.

—July 1, 1923

I am no philanthropist. I am hard to separate from money; if I killed two birds with one stone I would want the stone back.

—July 22, 1923

After that '28 election there was no holding 'em. They really did think they had "hard times" cornered once and for all. There was merger upon merger; get two non-paying things merged and then issue more stock to the public. Everywhere consolidation and holding companies.

And all these foreign loans, none too solid and every big consolidation not just the best investment. Big business sure got big, but it got big by selling stock and not by selling its product. No scheme was halted by the government as long as somebody would buy the stock. It could have been a scheme to deepen the Atlantic Ocean and the stock would have gone on the market.

—November 27, 1932

Just to be rich and nothing else is practically a disgrace nowadays.

—June 11, 1929

PROVERB ON WALL STREET: What Goes Up Musta Been Sent Up By Somebody.

— "Three Cheers," 1928

Our [stock] market is all cockeyed. Nothing seems to determine the worth of the stock but the fact that it was going up and that it hadn't reached a thousand yet and that there was no reason why it shouldn't keep on going till it did.

All you had to do was to buy and wait till the next morning and just pick up the paper and see how much you made—in print.

—November 24, 1929

Branch banks are all the go now. They realize they have got to bring the bank nearer the robber. He won't be annoyed by driving through traffic just to rob one bank.

—October 25, 1927

We can talk all the politics we want, but business rises above politics in this country.

— April 21, 1935

All the big financiers and writers are saying "good" values are worth as much as they ever were.

But that's the trouble—nobody knows what they ever were worth.

—November 9, 1929

There are more commissions paid out to stock salesmen than are ever collected by stock buyers.

—October 14, 1923

You can't sell a pair of shoes in New York without it's done through the Stock Exchange. I got an order in with a broker for ten subway tickets.

—December 6, 1928

The President called all Bankers in and they announced what their annual Gyp would be for the coming year. They agreed to be more careful in their loans, and see that the borrower dident buy a farm with it, as Agriculture was so uncertain. Try and get them to invest in some business where he could read the paper in the morning and see what he had. But it's great work, and I am just crazy about it. Viva confidence.

—December 1, 1929

Branch banks are all the go now. They realize they have got to bring the bank nearer the robber. He won't be annoyed by driving through traffic just to rob one bank.

—October 25, 1927

What's this investigation going to lead to, and will it do any good? Yes, it's going to be very educational [about] big business. It's going to show us just how big business got big. It got big according to law, but not according to Hoyle.

—May 30, 1933

A HOLDING COMPANY IS A **thing** WHERE YOU HAND AN ACCOMPLICE THE GOODS WHILE THE POLICEMAN **searches** YOU.

—March 13, 1935

It's not from any personal view that I am for abolishing banks. It's just that I don't think these boys realize what a menace they are. As far as being good fellows, personally, I heard old-timers talk down home in the Indian Territory, and they say that Jesse James and the Dalton boys were the most congenial men of their day too.

If you think it ain't a sucker game, why is your banker the richest man in your town?

—March 18, 1923

If a bank fails in China, they behead the man at the head of it that was responsible. If one fails over here, we write the men up in the magazines, as how they started poor, worked hard, took advantage of their opportunities (and depositors), and today are rated as "up in the millions."

If we beheaded all of ours that were responsible for failures, we wouldn't have enough people left to bury the heads.

—February 6, 1927

Every Senator knew in his heart but didn't have the nerve to say: before you start dealing out public funds, you should have first found out: "Have we enough money to give aid to every industry? If not, I am not going to give part of them a sandwich and leave the rest go hungry." But no, they didn't do that. They just started right in helping the bankers, so every man, woman and child in the U.S. thinks, and rightly so, that they have got as much right to get some sort of government aid. The bankers, the railroads, and big business got the first U.S. dole, and it will never be finished till the last [of our citizens] reach in and get theirs.

—February 12, 1933

All these big moneyed people, they are just like the underworld— they all know each other and kinder work together.

—June 2, 1928

You see the fellow that loaned the money is always better able to lose it, than the fellow that borrowed it. The fellow that borrowed it blows it in and never uses it for the cause that he borrowed it, but the fellow that loaned it, he never loaned all that he had, he only loaned what he could spare, so if he could spare that much, why, he didn't need this that he loaned.

—March 12, 1933

If the other fellow sells cheaper than you, it is called "dumping." 'Course, if you sell cheaper than him, that's "mass production."

—March 5, 1932

I guess there is no race of people that it is so universally agreed that they pulled a boner as the International bankers. [Now] our home bankers…are in bad through an over-expansion in good times, but the international one is in bad through malice aforethought. His devilment was premeditated. He knew he was loaning on no security, cause there is no security over there. He got his commission for peddling it out, so what does he care?

—April 3, 1932

OIL

IN SHORT, WILL ROGERS VIEWED the oil industry as a cross between a lottery and a Ponzi scheme:

> There has been at least one lawyer [in the petroleum industry] for every barrel that ever come out of the ground.
>
> You might wonder if they pay so much to lawyers how do they ever make anything out of oil. Foolish question! They don't make anything out of the oil. They only make money out of the stock they sell. You buy a share of oil stock and for every dollar you pay, sixty percent goes for lawyers' fees, thirty percent to over capitalization, and ten percent goes to the boring of a dry hole.
>
> [T]he lawyer has to make the lease....Then, if they happen to be leasing from the government, why they not only have to be lawyers but have to be political lawyers.
>
> Now, I bet a lot of you thought after the company had got the land leased, that the next thing to do was to hire a driller

to put the well down. But you are wrong again. You go out and get another lawyer to draw up the contract with the driller.

Then I bet you that you think the next step is to wait until you see whether you have oil or not. Say, don't make me laugh out Loud again. You don't wait for anything of the kind; you engage another lawyer to draw up some pretty oil stock paper with nice flowered edges. Looks like a marriage license only worse. Then you start selling the stock claiming that the Bohunk Oil Company are putting down a well on Smith 29, North East 40 of South West 80. Then if they do strike something, they shut it up and claim it was a duster.

Then you get another local lawyer who knows everyone around that neck of the woods, to go out and buy up or lease all of the adjoining land. Then when they get it all leased, they go back and pick the stopper out of this well, double the capitalization of stock under the direction of still another lawyer, and then they are in a position to investigate getting a lease from Persia or Yugoslavia.

———————————

You see it was our tribe of Cherokees that sold the original old Cherokee Strip. I think the Government only give us about a dollar an acre for it. We had it for hunting grounds, but we never knew enough to hunt oil on it. I can remember as a kid the payment we had, when the Government paid out about $320 apiece, I think it was.

The Cherokees are supposed to be the highest civilized Tribe there is and yet that's all we ever got in all our lifetime and sold a fortune in oil. Yet there was the Osages lived right by us and they get that much before breakfast every morning, and they are supposed to be uncivilized.

—May 4, 1930

Personally, I am glad that [the Senate committee investigating Teapot Dome] did unearth members of both parties, for if this thing had gone through showing no one but Republicans, it would have cast a reflection on the shrewdness of the Democratic Party. In other words, they would have looked rather dumb to be standing around with these oily shekels falling all around them and not opening their pockets to catch a few. For the American people are a very generous people and will forgive almost any weakness, with the possible exception of stupidity.

—February 24, 1924

There is a conference in Lausanne, where they are trying to talk Turkey out of some oil wells. Some nations go to war for gold, some nations for the territory, some to make the world safe for Democracy. But if you want to make a war with England, you show 'em an oil well.

—January 14, 1923

Is this a good tip, or ain't it? No business in the United States is as cockeyed as the oil business (and many States depend on it for their prosperity). If ever a business needed a dictator, it is them. It would be the biggest job held by a single man outside the President.

It must not be an oilman, for he is already linked with one side or the other. It's got to be a man that the whole oil industry knew is on the level, fearless, fair, seeking nothing but justice to thousands that produce oil and millions that use it.

—May 15, 1933

GIVE AN AMERICAN A **one-piece** BATHING SUIT, A HAMBURGER, AND FIVE GALLONS OF GASOLINE AND THEY ARE AS **tickled** AS A MOVIE STAR WITH A NEW DIVORCE.

—September 4, 1933

...I was telling you about Mosul, which is both a town and a province, which [England] wanted for twenty-five years. Now what does that signify to you? Get out your deductions!

Mosul must have had something they wanted!

You are right, Watson! What do you suppose Mosul had? Why Mosul must have had oil!

But why just for twenty-five years? Why not for life?

Because twenty-five years is about the life of an oil field. What would they want with it after the oil was gone?

—January 31, 1926

They struck oil on Navajos' land three years ago. I foolishly asked how often they get their payments for their oil royalty. Well, they hadn't any yet. They took a million of it to build a bridge across the Little Colorado River so tourists wouldn't have to drive so far around to see the Grand Canyon. The Navajos paid for the bridge and there has never been a Navajo crossed it yet.

—November 7, 1927

You know I never saw people moving around so much. Every one of us hustling from bank to bank, trying to renew notes. A man has to be careful nowadays or he will burn up more gasoline trying to get a loan than the loan is [worth]. One fellow paid the bank his interest out here the other day, and the police heard about it, followed him, and sure enough, he had been in some of the late robberies.

—May 17, 1932

YOU KNOW I NEVER HAD ANY KIND OF **diploma**. I NEVER FINISHED FROM ANYTHING. I ALWAYS DID WANT SOMETHING THAT LOOKED **important**. I NEVER EVEN HAD AN OIL SHARE.

—July 14, 1929

The idea that a tax on something keeps anybody from buying it, is a lot of hooey. They put it on gasoline all over the country and it hasn't kept a soul at home a single night or day. You could put a dollar a gallon on and still a pedestrian couldn't cross the street in safety without armor.

—March 17, 1932

[An oilman was out at the ranch] the other day. Said he was going to Washington where the oilmen were going to draw up a code of ethics. Everybody present had to laugh. If he had said the gangsters of America were drawing up a code of ethics, it wouldn't have sounded near as impossible.

—July 12, 1933

[I talk about many different things, but] I doubt I know any more about 'em than a boweevil—and I don't even know how to spell boweevil. But there is one subject that I do have a right smart sprinkling of knowledge on: I know the difference between good times and bad times is gasoline, and what goes with it.

—March 3, 1935

LABOR

BETTY ROGERS HAD GIVEN her husband's Christmas gift serious thought. Times were tough, the country was in a deep economic depression; this was no time to be wasteful, even though the Rogers family could well afford luxuries. These were the most lucrative years of Will Rogers's career. They lived in Pacific Palisades, California, on a several-hundred-acre ranch, had their own polo field, large stables for riding horses and polo ponies, private riding trails, a staff to look after the family, and the sizeable help needed to tend the horses and grounds. California would quickly revert to the desert from which it came if it were neglected for even a short time. Grass, flowers, shrubs, and trees would wither unless regularly watered. The monthly water bill at the ranch was one thousand dollars—an enormous amount during the Depression when a man's fair twelve-hour wage was five dollars—if, indeed, he had a job.

Just because Will was busier than ever was no reason to spend money pointlessly, Betty had thought when she bought the small tractor for her husband's Christmas gift. She was certain that the tractor could easily pay for itself by replacing three to four men on the work detail.

Will seemed very pleased with the present, but put it into the barn and did not use it, nor did he reduce the staff. On September 6, 1931, he explained in his weekly column:

"Machines are a great thing, but if one replaces a hundred men, it don't buy anything, it don't eat anything, while a hundred men spend their pay back for food, shelter, and hundreds of various commodities for themselves and their families. Folks got to have work."

———

Mr. Gompers[12] has spent his life trying to keep Labor from working too hard, and he has succeeded beyond his own dreams.

—December 28, 1924

I see where the coal strike was settled in the usual way—with the public paying more for coal.

—1920

See where one strike ended. Nobody won anything but you always word the agreement in such way that it looks like both sides gained something.

China has a word...it's called "face"...How-Can-I-Do-Nothing-And-Still-Make-It-Look-Like-I-Did-Something?

—June 17, 1934

Labor leaders don't do much laboring after they are able to lead.

—January 21, 1928

England elected a Labor government, but nobody has ever accused ours of doing a tap of work.

—June 5, 1929

Every holiday ought to be named Labor Day. If we could ever get vacation down to where you wasn't any more tired on the day one was over than on a regular workday, it would be wonderful.

—September 4, 1933

By the way, a good stiff sales tax on hamburgers this Labor Day would pay our national Debt.

—September 4, 1933

Labor. We can confidentially report to our clients that labor is not laboring. As to the cause of labor not laboring, it's generally rumored around here among our sources of information that labor is not laboring because labor hasent got a job.

—November 12, 1933

Manufacturers have associations for their mutual betterment, bankers have associations to see how they can help each other out, and there is nothing fairer than workmen having unions for their mutual benefit.

—August 19, 1934

Did you see what the Senate voted for yesterday? That's a week's work was to consist of thirty hours—six hours a day, for five days?

I doubt very much if the [working] people...will agree to an increase in time of work like that. We stick to the old American principle of only working when the boss is looking.

—April 7, 1933

A strike should be the very last means, for it is like war. It falls on those who had nothing to do with calling it.

—August 6, 1933

Labor Day is set by Act of Congress, I suppose. Everything we do nowadays is either by, or against Acts of Congress.

How Congress knew anything about Labor is beyond us.

—September 1, 1929

All strikes that deal in a commodity are hurting nobody but the people that use and want that commodity.

—January 14, 1928

I asked Mussolini about his No-Strike Plan. He told me that he had formed Labor, Capital, and Government into a trust and everything has to be submitted to this body. It is against the law to strike or cause a lockout.

He said a strike is just like a fight out here in the public square that is crowded with people and two men started shooting at each other. Everybody gets hit more than the two men shooting at each other.

—July 31, 1926

STATES AND CITIES

BECAUSE OF HIS HUMBLE ORIGINS and open mind Rogers could empathize with folks from any part of the country. However, he was not immune from the tendency of Americans to be biased in favor of their own town or state. In his case, Claremore, Oklahoma, his hometown, was usually cast in a favorable light (with a little tongue in cheek) and Oklahoma generally got a pass among the states. California, where he lived much of the time, came in for a lot of kidding, but he stood up for it when Floridians made unflattering comparisons between California and Florida.

Big cities such as New York (where Rogers lived for many years) and Chicago came in for special ribbing, usually related to bootlegging, gangsters, and crime in the streets.

The bigotry and ignorance of the South in the early-twentieth century attracted the occasional comment as well.

However much of Rogers's regional humor merely served to point out, that despite our many differences, American are remarkable similar everywhere, are faced by similar problems, and enjoy similar things.

We got a new police chief in New York. He has the cops so scared that they are arresting traffic instead of directing it.

—January 13, 1929

Jimmy Walker, the mayor of New York, called in a hundred prominent citizens to discuss graft with him. A man, naturally, wouldn't call in a hundred poor men to discuss graft, as they would have no technical knowledge of the subject.

These hundred met and adjourned without adopting any resolution to either halt, or increase it. It seemed everyone was satisfied as it is.

—September 14, 1930

We had quite a Panic here the other day in New York, in the Subway; several people were trampled on and crushed. The cause of the trouble was that someone hollered out: "Here's a vacant seat."

—May 23, 1925

Some guy went over Niagara Falls yesterday and run Coolidge and Hoover off the front page. Shows what hard work, perseverance, and taking advantage of your opportunities will do for you.

—July 5, 1928

The biggest Marathon race we have in this country finished up here [in Boston] today; and an old boy from Canada won it, because he never owned a Ford and didn't know how to run one. Outsiders won everything.

We ride good, but we get out of wind walking to the garage.

—April 19, 1929

Jimmy Walker knew Mr. Hoover did things by committees, say six or eight, so he called a hundred and told 'em something should be done about small graft in New York.

Small graft was getting the city a bad name and it would eventually lose its reputation for doing things on a big scale.

—September 4, 1930

A lot of you states have had a lot of trouble during the last seven weeks because your legislatures have met. There's nothing will upset a state economic condition like a legislature. It's better to have termites in your house than the legislature.

—March 31, 1935

If you have ever dealt with a Vermonter you know they are not giving away any eleven billion dollars. Even for eleven dollars they would go to war with you.

—May 29, 1925

I see that all the papers have been commenting on the novel way by which the State of Nevada executed a man for committing murder.

Well, the novelty of that was that a prisoner was executed in *any* way for committing murder!

—June 6, 1930

Robbery statistics from all cities were shown today. (They can show the statistics, but no robbers.)

We don't want to be accused of bragging as usual, but Los Angeles was second, right behind Detroit. We will catch 'em next month if we can only dig up some money to be robbed of.

—December 1, 1930

I flew into Oklahoma today, just one day after our new Governor was christened. He has been in twenty-four hours now with no talk of impeachment, so it looks like we have a novelty in there at last.

—January 13, 1931

Our new Governor is going to help Oklahoma's unemployment problem by not releasing any more prisoners. If we had everybody back in jail that was in, and that ought to be in, why, we would have to borrow outside hands.

—January 13, 1930

Mayor Bill Thompson today said he was going to try and do better and make Chicago the happiest city in America to live in....He made it seem so beautiful, everybody is trading their machine guns for hymn books.

—July 27, 1928

Florida has the longest seacoast of any state. [They] have 1,145 miles, and that is a hundred miles more than California has.

Now what has a long coastline got to do with the quality of a state?...Siberia has quite a mess of seacoast, but I have never heard of any emigration—that is, voluntary—on account of their seacoast.

—May 29, 1926

Every guy thinks the first time he sees anything that that is the first time it ever existed. I will never forget the first time I went to St. Louis, I thought sure I was the first one to find it.

—March 13, 1927

I SEE WHERE AN ALDERMAN GOT **robbed** HERE IN NEW YORK. I THOUGHT IT WAS AN UNWRITTEN LAW THAT CROOKS DID NOT **bother** EACH OTHER.

—January 16, 1925 or 1926

This murderer out here in California confessed, so that means a long, drawn-out trial. It's going to be a fight to the finish between the psychiatrists and the photographers.

—November 23, 1928

HEADLINE SAYS: "Thirteen Bankers in Detroit Indicted!"
You would think Detroit was a bigger town than that.

—June 6, 1934

We took California away from Mexico the next year after we found it had gold.

When the gold was all gone, we tried to give it back, but Mexico was too foxy for us.

—September 9, 1932

This is primary day in New York City to see who will be the Democratic candidate for Mayor.

I don't see why they don't have the Governor for Mayor. He could hold both jobs. He could run this town in the evenings. And come to think of it, that is when New York City needs running. Everybody is asleep here all day.

—September 13, 1925

The snow was so deep today in Chicago that the crooks could only shoot a tall man.

—January 9, 1930

Chicago is kinder like the Stock Market. It has been away off par lately but it got back to normal yesterday. They machine-gunned seven.

—June 2, 1930

HEADLINE SAYS: "Chicago Electrocuted Four Gangsters!"

Their limousine must have crossed a live wire.

—October 16, 1931

I am just entering Iowa. I haven't been here in years, not since it moved to Long Beach, California. I am looking forward with great anxiety to seeing the birthplace of ninety percent of Southern California's native sons. California just uses Iowa as a sort of hatchery.

—November 8, 1925

IN HOLLYWOOD YOU WILL SEE THINGS AT NIGHT THAT ARE **fast enough** TO BE IN THE OLYMPICS IN THE DAYTIME.

—May 1, 1932

Everything is in California....We maintain more freak religions and cults than all of the rest of the world combined. Just start anything out here and if it is cuckoo enough, you will get followers.

—December 8, 1929

Never a day passes in New York without some innocent bystander being shot. You just stand around this town long enough and be innocent, and somebody is going to shoot you.

One day there was four innocent people shot here. That's the best shooting ever done in this town. Hard to find four innocent people in New York.

—May 31, 1923

I have been in old Philadelphia for a couple of weeks and you would be surprised at the life the old Girl is showing. Philadelphia is trying to become known outside somnambulistic circles....It's been fairly well established that Washington slept here in not only one, but various beds.

Washington crossed the Delaware (with everyone rowing but him) somewhere near here....I don't remember whether he crossed it to get to, or away from Philadelphia.

—May 19, 1929

Am down in Old Virginia, the mother of Presidents when we thought Presidents had to be aristocrats. Since we got wise to the limitation of aristocrats, Virginia has featured their ham over their Presidential timber.

—January 31, 1927

I see where New York is going to make their nightclubs close at three in the morning and the people are kicking about it. Well, I say they ought to close 'em. Anybody that can't get drunk by [3 A.M.], ain't trying.

—Lecture 1926

I am [leaving California for New York]. I do so with great regret. I know that I am exchanging the sub-division for the subway, and one single California flea for a billion Long Island mosquitoes. I am leaving a city where English is the dominant tongue, to return to a city where it is seldom heard and never understood. I leave from the land where the movies are made to return to the land where the bills are paid.

—May 25, 1924

Here in Alaska the hospitality and generosity of a trapper, or a man that lives away out, would put us to absolute shame. On the mainland…we pass folks every day—every hour—that we could help, but we don't do it.

Here they would mush through the winter—50 below—for days to help a friend. We think they punish animals. We punish humans, only we don't think so.

—September 8, 1935 (Published posthumously)

[CHICAGO] BOX SCORE FOR TODAY: "Died of gunshot and other natural...causes: 13; wounded 23.

Bad weather kept outdoor shooting down to a minimum."

—November 23, 1926

You Texans have a queer way of running your primaries. Of course, the primary is the election in the South, they won't let a Republican eat at the same table with folks.

—December 13, 1925

ARKANSAS **voted** LAST TUESDAY AGAINST EVOLUTION AND REPUBLICANS. THEY DON'T WANT ANYTHING **taught** ABOUT EITHER SUBJECT IN THEIR SCHOOLS.

—November 11, 1928

Florida claims that this year alone, oranges brought them $15 million! Well, in California, that would just about pay for the labels on the ones we shipped.

—May 29, 1926

Florida claims their grapefruit sells for about ten million dollars a year and they think it is the best in the world.

We in California use the juice of their grapefruits as fly spray. We had no idea anyone ate them.

—May 29, 1926

[Vermont] is what you would call a "hard-boiled state." The principal ingredients are granite, rock salt, and Republicans. The last being the hardest of the three.

—March 19, 1925

The Supreme Court of Tennessee…has just ruled that you other States can come from whoever or whatever you want to, but they want it on record that they come from mud only.

—January 17, 1927

HOLIDAYS

ROGERS FELT THAT HOLIDAYS in the twentieth century had drifted away from their original purpose: to commemorate something or someone truly important, to rest from work, and to have some fun. Instead, Americans were confronted with occasions that seemed to be designed to market products. After these modern holidays, people who survived were generally more exhausted than if they had worked. Christmas was a good example:

> [At Christmas we] are buying a lot of stuff and giving it to folks that don't understand why you was so half-witted as to get that particular object. It is the last thing on earth they would want....Of course the whole thing started in a fine spirit. It was to give happiness to the young...no matter what they dug out [from their stockings] it was great....It was

a great day; the presents were inexpensive and received with much joy and gratification.

As somebody who was part Native American, Rogers also had particular trouble with holidays such as Columbus Day and Thanksgiving that celebrated something that was favorable for Americans of European ancestry but not necessarily favorable for the original inhabitants of the continent.

This is President's Day. We generally recognize anything by a week. We have Apple Week, Prune Week, Don't Get Hurt by an Automobile Week. So somebody had the bright idea and they said: "If prunes are worth a week, the President ought to be worth something, anyhow."
They compromised on a Day.

—April 30, 1933

All the casualties are not in yet, but it seems to have been a mighty quiet May Day. Heretofore the Reds have battled with police, but this year everybody is "beefing" so that you can't tell Reds from taxpayers.

—May 1, 1931

When the Fourth of July and a Sunday come together there just ain't anything to do on Monday but send flowers.

Fireworks killed and maimed everybody that had a match. Riptides in the ocean just wait for a holiday to get their quota, and autos got what was left. About the only sure way to keep from being hurt on the Fourth of July is to participate in one of our heavyweight prizefights.

—July 6, 1931

Well, Xmas spirit is over now. Everybody can get back to their natural dispositions....

Christmas will never be a real charity benefit till we learn to eat those Xmas cards. If we spent as much with the Salvation Army as we do the telegraph companies every Xmas, why the poor would be fat all winter.

But we can all go back to work with a clear conscience. We fed 'em Xmas and New Year's; now all the poor have to do is just to fill in the few meals till next Xmas.

—December 25, 1928

After reading the casualty list every Fifth of July morning, one learns that we have killed more people celebrating our independence than we lost fighting for it.

—July 22, 1923

We been awfully busy here today in Boston, celebrating Bunker Hill. Daniel Webster made the most famous Bunker Hill address. He spoke good English, too. You give me a chance to write my own dictionary and make a word mean anything I want it to, and I will show you some English.

—June 17, 1930

This is Mother's Day. Of course the mother I know most about is the mother of our little group. She has been for twenty-two years trying to raise to maturity four children, three by birth and one by marriage.

While she hasn't done a good job, the poor soul has done all that mortal human could do with the material she has had to work with.

—May 11, 1930

My wife just reminded me that this was Mother's Day. Never having been a mother, that didn't impress me so much. My wife is not my mother, that's for her children to think of, not me. My own poor mother passed on long ago, before anyone thought of honoring them with a day, we didn't even send 'em flowers.

—Notes

I'm celebrating Mother's Day by giving "Ma" Rogers a vacation. Picked her a white desert flower and walked her for several miles through the celebrated Carlsbad Caverns. I thought the biggest hole in the ground was when you was drilling for oil and struck a dry hole. But this is bigger even than that. It's just like the Grand Canyon with a roof over it.

—May 1, 1931

This Sunday is Mother's Day—a beautiful thought, whoever started it. Now what could please your mother more, either living or dead, than to mail one dollar to your nearest Red Cross for the flood sufferers.[13]

Even if you have given, give again, just because it's in memory of your mother.

—May 5, 1927

All of you know that this is Mother's Day, but did all of you know that tomorrow is Hospital Day? The only way that we know that our civilization has advanced in this country is by our splendid hospitals. It is the birthday of Florence Nightingale, the founder of modern nursing.

It is fine to remember the well, but it is the sick that really need it, so do something for somebody tomorrow at a hospital.

—May 11, 1930

As this is written it's nearing the end of Mother's Day. It was a beautiful thought these florists had to propose this day. I propose a Father's Day. No flowers, no fuss, just let him use the car himself and go where he wants to.

But he will never live to see such a contented day.

—May 12, 1930

You know, there ought to be some kind of a star given to any woman that can live with a comedian.

Now that little compliment ought to repay for the flowers that I forgot to get on Mother's Day.

—May 11, 1930

We really ought to have celebrated today, the Fifth of July, because of the small number of people that lost their lives yesterday, the Fourth.

They must be getting more harmless powder.

—July 5, 1929

I said yesterday Daniel Webster wrote the dictionary. Well, these Harvardites have been calling me up before daylight, telling me it was Noah Webster and not Daniel.

How was I to know? I never read the book.

—June 18, 1930

Fireworks was sure popping last night. The Fourth has turned out to be a national benefit for the du Ponts.

—July 5, 1928

Another Decoration Day passed and Mr. Abraham Lincoln's 300-word Gettysburg Address was not dethroned. I would try and imitate its brevity, if nothing else. Of course, Lincoln had the advantage—he had no foreign policy to put over. He didn't even have a foreign policy. That's why he is still Lincoln.

—May 31, 1927

If Columbus had landed at Galveston and marched inland to Santa Fe, New Mexico, he would have been met by the "Cliff Dwellers Commercial Club," a delegation of modern "Redmen of the World" and the Aztecs Rotary.

Columbus would have remarked: "Pardon me, Gentlemen! I didn't discover a country; I am just over here paying my respects from a young country to an older one."

—March 13, 1927

Christopher Columbus was about the first of the foreigners to start coming over, but somebody would have found America, even if he hadn't, for you couldn't hardly get around without running into it.

Being an Indian, I don't mind telling you personally, *I am sorry he ever found us.* The discovery has been of no material benefit to us, outside of losing all our land. I am proud to say that I have never yet seen a statue in Oklahoma to him.

—August 1, 1925

The Columbus celebration has rather an added significance to Los Angeles, as they want to celebrate the good fortune of his landing on the Atlantic instead of the Pacific side, because if he had landed out here, he never would have gone back even to tell the queen.

He would have stayed right here and nobody would have ever known about him.

—July 1, 1923

I have always had quite an admiration for Christopher Columbus. He beat the Immigration Laws and when he landed in some islands he was about as near to America as he was when he left Spain but they stretched a point and gave him the best of it and said he landed here.

Spain and Italy are having an argument over which country he really come from. Spain claims that he might have been born in Italy but it was without his consent. The Italians claim that when he died, Spain buried him in their country without his consent.

—August 1, 1926

Some of the writers are having a little trouble scraping up a reason for Thanksgiving this year. Some think we ought to skip a year and put on a big one in '31.

The original idea of the day was to give thanks for the "bountiful harvest." Well, the "bountiful harvest" is the very thing that's the matter with us: too much wheat, too much corn, too much cotton, too much beef, too much production of everything.

So we are going through a unique experience. We are the first nation to starve to death in a storehouse that's overfilled with everything we want.

—November 26, 1930

> TOMORROW IS THANKSGIVING DAY, FOR NO **reason** AT ALL. THE MORE TURKEY YOU EAT AT DINNER THE LESS HASH YOU WILL BE **bothered** WITH THE REST OF THE MONTH.
>
> —November 24, 1926

This is Thanksgiving. It was started by the Pilgrims, who would give thanks every time they killed an Indian and took more of his land. As years went by and they had all his land, they changed it into a day to give thanks for the bountiful harvest, when the boll-weevil and the protective tariff didn't remove all cause for thanks.

—November 23, 1927

Thanksgiving is right on us and we got to do some thinking over just what we got to give thanks for. 'Course we are glad to be living. I guess we will just give thanks that we had invested in land, instead of Wall Street, even if we can't sell the land; we can at least walk on it.

Still, I got some you can't walk on unless you have Divine power.

—November 24, 1929

In the days of its founders they were willing to give thanks for mighty little (for mighty little was all they expected). But now neither government nor nature can give enough but what we think it's too little.

Those old boys in the Fall of the year, if they could gather in a few pumpkins, potatoes, and some corn for the winter, they was in a thanking mood. But if we can't gather in a new Buick, a new radio, a tuxedo, and some government relief, why we feel like the world is agin us.

—November 28, 1934

Well, President Coolidge went South to Old Virginia for Thanksgiving, but you notice he didn't go there till after it had gone Republican. He used to spend it in Massachusetts, but not lately.

With all our boasted prosperity I don't see that we are better off. The old turkey hash showed up as usual today and will be with us the next few days, just the same as it did when we were poor.

—November 30, 1928

That liberty that we got 159 years ago Thursday was a great thing, but they ought to pass a law that we could only celebrate it every one hundred years, for at the rate of accidents yesterday we won't have enough people to celebrate it every year.

And the speeches? Did you read them? Never was as much politics indulged in under the guise of "freedom and liberty." They was five percent what George Washington did, and ninety-five percent what the speaker intended to do.

—July 5, 1935

Well, this is Armistice Day and we talk about how terrible nations are and how they are about to fight all the time. But do you know, they have done pretty well, I think, sixteen years is a long time for all these hundreds of breeds of cats to live together and not have a fight.

—Notes

This day, Armistice Day, is no doubt the greatest day in all the world history. When you think that a half-dozen men could sit down and casually sign a pact to stop millions of men from killing each other.

But if they don't stop these guys making speeches on Armistice Day, why, we are liable to have the same war over again, only worse.

—November 11, 1929

> IF ARMISTICE DAY HAD **stopped** SPEECHES, IT WOULD HAVE DONE MORE THAN TO HAVE STOPPED THE WAR, FOR SPEECHES IS WHAT **starts** THE NEXT WAR. IT'S NOT ARMAMENT; IT'S ORATORY.
>
> —November 11, 1929

I called on a businessman at his office the other day, when the girl outside his office phoned him, he said for me to come right in. The girl looked astonished at his quick reply and said to me: "Why you can get in there as quick as a bootlegger." But I do sincerely hope that the holiday booze has by now finished with its spring drive.

—January 4, 1925

While we are merging everything in the world that has no relation to each other, why not merge Christmas, Fourth of July, Ground Hog Day, Thanksgiving Day, Labor Day, Halloween, New Years, and April's Fool all into one glorious day that would give everybody a chance to get some work done during the year.

And look at the speeches, sermons, and turkey it would save.

—December 24, 1929

This is our last day of grace. Tomorrow we are obliged to read the usual New Year's prosperity applesauce by our same prominent men, who are always rich enough to see a great year coming up. And to show you they don't know any more about it than Clara Bow,[14] last year they had their usual hokum predictions, and in October we lost half as much as it cost to put on the war.

—December 30, 1929

Well, I see where the Holiday Booze has started in on its Spring Drive. It's getting so Xmas kills more people than it makes happy. I used to think it was the Bootleggers that were the ones responsible for Prohibition, but I think the Undertakers are behind it stronger than the Bootleggers.

—December 18, 1924

LATIN AMERICA

IN 1928, WILL ROGERS WAS OFF on another trip. Unofficially, the visit was intended to help improve lukewarm relations between the United States and its neighbor, Mexico. There, he was received by Mexico's former President and was his guest of honor at an informal dinner at which he addressed Mexican legislators and important members of Mexico's foremost families.

As was his style, Rogers mixed humor and truth:

> Pass a law to make your rich Mexican invest at least half the money he gets out of his own country back into it again. You have more money in this City invested in French dresses and perfumes than you have in the Country in plows. It's not American confidence you are looking for, it's Mexican confidence.
>
> Make your rich—every time they send a child to Paris to learn 'em to talk French—make them send one to Sonora

to learn to talk Yaqui. They are the ones you have to live and get along with, not the French. You got more imported cars here than you have milk cows.

I was up and paid a call on our friend here, Mr. Estrada, Secretary of State, today, and he got out a wonderful bottle and gave me a swig of what he called Mexican Hospitality. It was Tequila. Then he asked me how I liked Mexico. Why, with one more swig of that Tequila a person would have been fond of Siberia.

The only trouble with Spanish is, the Verbs have too many endings.

I just want to find one thing before going home—I want to find what makes every Mexican a Guitar player.

Now if I was looking for comedy in Government, I dident have to come here to Mexico. I could have stayed at home. I come down here to laugh with you and not at you.

Just been reading about Augusto Sandino[15] down in Nicaragua. As to whether he was a George Washington, or a Jesse James, that's for his own people to judge.

There is one thing that he and I agree on, and that was that American armed forces had no right down there.

—February 22, 1934

At one time our Marines had Sandino surrounded at a town called Los Quas Ka Jasbo. But nobody knew where Los Quas Ka Jasbo was. They should have caught him. They had him hemmed in between the Atlantic and the Pacific, and all they had to do was stop up both ends.

—August 5, 1923

It does seem good to be able to read of the revolutions in Argentina, Peru, and Brazil, and not read where "American Marines have landed and have the situation well in hand."

—September 8, 1930

There is no reason why we shouldent get on with this Country. You have lots of things down here that we want, and as long as we get 'em, why, we ought to hit it off great.

—June 9, 1928

I had me an impromptu speech that I had only worked on steady for four days. Well, here was my oral note to the former Mexican President and his Cabinet and our Ambassador and the others.

I didn't come here to tell you that Mexico needed American Capital. Mexico needs Mexican Capital.

—June 9, 1928

At this recent Pan-American Conference, the President made a good speech. He didn't say that we would do anything for these countries, but on the other hand he didn't say we would do anything against them.

—January 16, 1928

Been reading President Hoover's speech yesterday to the Puerto Ricans. The keynote of the speech was "the rapid increase in population of the islanders."

He was in a tough spot. He didn't know whether to compliment 'em on being a virile race or condemn 'em for making the usual American mistake of overproduction. You see, there is not enough jobs there to take care of this increase, so what he tactfully wanted to impart to them was to control themselves till industry was on a par with affection.

He finally left the whole thing and departed for the Virgin Islands, where he hoped conditions would be better regulated.

—March 25, 1931

Wouldn't it be great if Mexico started electing by the ballot instead of by the bullet, and us electing by the ballot instead of by the bullion.

—September 2, 1928

There is one thing about a Latin American country. No matter who is running it, they are always run the same.

—September 6, 1933

I TELL YOU, THE **difference** OF OUR EXCHANGE OF PEOPLE WITH MEXICO IS: THEY **send** WORKMEN HERE TO WORK, WHILE WE SEND AMERICANS TO **work** MEXICO.

—June 27, 1925

Secretary of State Kellogg sent a diplomatic note to Mexico, saying something like: "America is getting tired of your nation not paying us for land taken by the revolutionists from some of our respectful citizens. Remember, Mexico is on trial before the eyes of the world."

Mexico replied that they were paying taxes in Mexico and that, as a matter of fact the eyes of the world were on the dollar bill, and that outside of the oil interests and Americans who want to make money out of Mexico the rest of the world's eyes don't even know Mexico exists.

—June 27, 1925

Q: Why did the President think we were trusted in South America?

A: He had never been there.

Q: Was you ever in South America?

A: I was.

Q: Was you trusted?

A: Yes, as long as I paid in advance, I was.

Q: Do you think America stands very good with all the other countries of the world?

A: We stand alone.

Q: What would foreign countries do if we needed help?

A: I think they would hold a celebration.

Q: Do you think any of them would help us out?

A: Well, offhand I can't think of a single one that would, unless it might be Wisconsin.

—January 31, 1926

You give Ecuador England's navy and right away Ecuador's ambassador would be seated next to the President at official functions.

—April 7, 1929

Pancho Villa[16] died what's called a natural death in Mexico. He was shot in the back.

—August 5, 1923

We started to pay attention to our neighbors to the South. Up to now our calling cards to Mexico and Central America had been a gunboat, or a bunch of violets shaped like Marines.

—May 12, 1928

America has a commission down there, trying to have Mexico to recognize us. We have changed so in the last few years that very few nations know us now. The way we are trying to make up with Mexico, they must have struck more oil lately.

—August 5, 1923

I brag on Mexico. I'm always blowin' about Mexico. I like Mexico. I like their Mexicans. Folks say: "Why, Will, you know that Mexico is run all wrong!" Well, that don't make any difference to me. It's their country. Let 'em run it like they want to.

—October 14, 1934

I am having dinner tonight with General Obregon, the sole surviving candidate of all Mexican Parties. Just think, if you had to eat with every presidential candidate of both political Parties at home, you would be eating out the rest of your life.

—December 9, 1927

I see where America and Mexico had a joint earthquake. That's the only thing I ever heard we split fifty-fifty with Mexico.

—January 2, 1927

There is no reason why we shouldn't get on with Mexico. You have lots of things down here that we want, and as long as we get 'em, why, we ought to hit it off great.

—June 9, 1928

I guess a Nicaraguan thinks a Ford, a machine gun, and a bevy of Marines is our only three products we make.

—December 1929

If we could get out of there and let Nicaragua alone, they might like us by the time we got ready to build the canal through their country.

—January 4, 1928

What right have the Marines got settling an election in Nicaragua? I thought even at home our Army and Navy was supposed to never enter politics. Evidently our Army and Navy have to go to South America to get into politics.

—December 5, 1925

Every time we pick up a paper "The American Marines have landed in Nicaragua!" There has been more Marines landed in Nicaragua than there has been at the Brooklyn Navy Yard.

How in the world did we find out where Nicaragua is, anyway?

—December 5, 1926

Advice can get you in more trouble than a gun can. I just don't want somebody telling me how to run my business, or my country. I want to ruin it myself without outside aid, and that's especially true of these Latin lands.

The minute there is any trouble in any Latin American country, that should be the tip right there for us to crawl in a hole and not even be allowed to poke our head out till it was all over, for as sure as we could see it we would either be in it or offering advice. We can't help it; it's just second nature with us. We mean well, but the better we mean the worse we get in.

—August 20, 1933

The best thing to do with these Latin American countries is to get out, let 'em alone, and then sell things cheaper and better than any other nation. Then we don't have to worry about relations and goodwill.

—April 13, 1931

We send Marines to Nicaragua to tell them how to run an election and missionaries to China. No wonder we are funny to the rest of the world.

—April 4, 1927

NICARAGUA **voted** THE OTHER DAY NOT TO HAVE US SUPERVISE THEIR ELECTION, BUT THAT'S NOT OFFICIAL AS WE DIDN'T **supervise** THAT VOTE.

—March 23, 1928

Tomorrow is Pan-American Day! We are celebrating it by rushing two cruisers to Nicaragua.

—April 13, 1931

SLOGANS FOR OUR LATEST WAR:
Join the Navy and try and help America find Nicaragua!
Let's make Nicaragua free for 100-percent Americans to live in.

—December 28, 1928

Senator Brookhart[17] has just been down at Panama and he was shocked and said the people down there were "just wallowing in sin."

So the people of Panama asked me to come down to offset Brookhart and I kinder wanted to see and perhaps join the wallowing.

—April 12, 1931

Us up home, we just can't understand Latin politics. The only time they ever get to cheer is when one side overturns the other; then they get to cheer mighty fast.

—April 15, 1931

I am down here in Argentina; Buenos Aires, to be exact. Like all countries down here, the President is just in from day to day. He may be on the same plane with me, going out.

—October 18, 1932

An Argentine President visited Brazil. He went there on an Argentine battleship, was met by Brazilian cruisers and seventy-five fighter planes.

All this, mind you, on a good-will trip.

—October 8, 1933

We got the wrong impression of those Latin American revolutions. They was raised on 'em down there. They love 'em. It's their only relaxation.

Sure, people get killed sometimes, if it is a first-class "A" revolution. In fact, they may lose 'bout as many as we lose over a weekend by trying to pass somebody on a curve.

—December 6, 1933

The first country to question us on the worth of our fifty-nine-cent dollar is Panama. We are supposed to pay 'em for killing their mosquitoes and putting an irrigation ditch from one ocean to the other through their property. They say we are to pay in gold.

It would be a good joke on 'em if we just picked up our canal and come home.

—March 1, 1934

EUROPE

IT IS TRULY REMARKABLE TO NOTE Will Rogers's insight: He not only correctly diagnosed the political international scene, but he also had the ability to correctly draw conclusions. This was not only true in those countries he knew well, but even those he visited for the first time and in which he spent only a few days.

It would be wrong to paraphrase Rogers's opinions, as he had voiced them in the last century. Let us report what he wrote on August 26, 1926, in the series of articles called "More Letters of a Self-Made Diplomat to his President":

> Dear President Coolidge: Well, I have been gathering up a lot of facts and I am just about in shape to report.
>
> France and England think just as much of each other as two rival bands of Chicago Bootleggers. Italy went to bat on the side of France in the last Series, but that was just because

Austria was on the opposite side. A Frenchman and an Italian love each other just about like Minneapolis and St. Paul. Spain and France have the same regard for each other as Fort Worth and Dallas. Spain feels that they fought the Riffs for four years and then France come in and got all the best land at the settlement.

Russia hates everybody so bad it would take her a week to pick out the one she hates most. Poland is rarin' to fight somebody, or go up and annex Lithuania. Turkey has been laying off three months now without any war, and Peace is just about killing them. Bulgaria is feeding an Army and deriving no benefits from it whatever. Greece has some open time that they are trying to fill in. They will take on anybody but Turkey; they are about cured of them. Czecho-Slovakia is a new country, and they feel that a war would just about give them the proper prestige. Japan is filling up Chinese Manchuria with Japs and copping it away from China so fast that Russian interests are menaced there; and Russia is doing all they can to populate that end of Russia with Emigrants, for they know that sooner or later these two will have to tangle.

Mussolini is raising five hundred thousand children every year, and needs somewhere to stake 'em out. So that means Italy sooner or later has got to go out and fight for it. They won't do it now because this Guy is too wise, but he will when he thinks they are ready.

Portugal would like to join somebody in a war just to make them forget their own troubles. Holland just sets there and greases her windmills and sells butter and eggs and cheese to the Kaiser. Norway, Sweden and Denmark are apparently getting on pretty good; but you call a Swede a Dane, or get any of the three of them mixed up, and you better reach for your hat.

Everybody talks about how we are hated. Well, when the discussion would gradually come to the Shylocks, as we had been christened, why, I would just casually, of course, admit that we were a band of highbinders, and were just waiting to get England or France up a back alley and knock 'em in the head and get what little they had left; and while they were discussing jubilantly the subject of our unpopularity I would, in order to keep up the conversation and not change the subject, just nonchalantly remark, "Will you enumerate to me, in their natural order, the number of Nations that you people can call bosom friends?"

—August 26, 1926

HEADLINE IN THE PAPER SAYS: "Europe Criticizes United States!"

Well, if memory serves me right, we haven't complimented them lately ourselves.

—January 27, 1924

Been reading editorials on President Coolidge's debt and armament speech. Several papers have asked, "What would Europe do if we were in difficulties and needed help?"...Europe would hold a celebration.

—November 13, 1928

Perhaps you have had it hinted to you, that we stand in Europe about like a Horse Thief. Now I want to report to you that that is not so. It is what you call "erroneous." We don't stand like a Horse Thief abroad. Whoever told you we did is flattering us. We don't stand as good as a Horse Thief.

—August 26, 1926

It looks to me like the last war ought to be the greatest example against any future wars. What I mean by that is the winners are the losers. I have been in every Nation that was humorously supposed to have won the war, and then last I visited Germany, which is humorously referred to as the loser, and I want to tell you that if the next war is to be anything like the last one I wouldn't give you a five-cent piece to win it. Wars strike me as being the only game in the world where there is absolutely no winner—everybody loses.

—August 26, 1926

Americans have one particular trait that they need never have any fear of some other Nation copping, and that is, we are the only people that will go where we know we are absolutely not wanted.

—January 8, 1927

Well, I see where France has been acting up again about their war debt to us. A man made a speech against paying the debt, and the other members of Council of Deputies all cheered for an hour. Now what is the use of kidding ourselves? We know that they don't want to pay it. They don't even feel like they owe it. Any person or any nation will break a neck for each other if they think that is appreciated. But the thing about this French thing is not the money. They don't even in their own hearts appreciate, or even like us.

I would say to France, "You don't seem to think you owe us anything. What we did for you, you think we owed you. Now if it wasn't worth anything, why, let it go. But, listen, if we wasn't worth anything in this War, why, don't expect us in the next."

—February 1, 1925

America has a great habit of always talking about protecting American interests in some foreign country. Protect 'em at home! There is more American interests right here than anywhere.

—June 28, 1925

I looked for combinations that were friendly toward each other and have yet to find two—unless it was Latvia up toward the Arctic Ocean and Madagascar down on the Indian Ocean. They have no particular grievance against each other but they will have as soon as they find where each other are.

—October 2, 1926

> ## IF I WAS ENGLAND I WOULD give IRELAND HOME RULE, AND reserve THE MOTION PICTURE RIGHTS.
>
> —1920

England had an earthquake yesterday. Now there is a cricket match going on here that has been for three months—one game!

The earthquake didn't even wake up the spectators

—August 16, 1926

That's one good thing about European nations: They can't hate you so bad they wouldn't use you.

—March 31, 1935

Ireland is another pet of mine. If it's run cockeyed that don't make any difference to me. I like it. And they run it.

—October 14, 1934

Why don't we send Marines to France? They was throwing rocks at us over there all last summer, and we never said a word?

Well, that was all right. If anyone goes anywhere they ain't wanted, let 'em get hit.

—December 5, 1926

I bet you right now that if somebody could scare up an egg layin' contest in Czechoslovakia and if America could find out where it was, we would send more delegates and lay less eggs than any nation in the whole hen house.

—April 6, 1930

A guy named Hitler[18] has Germany like Capone has Chicago.

—October 16, 1930

Americans spent $700 million to be insulted in Europe last summer, and they could have got it done for half the money here.

—January 8, 1927

Been reading a lot lately about that guy Hitler, in Germany, that's getting quite a following. He advocates forgetting everything connected with the peace treaty and starting all over new.

And that is about what will happen in a few years.

—September 29, 1930

Papers all state Hitler is trying to copy Mussolini.[19] Looks to me like it's the Ku Klux Klan that he is copying. He don't want to be Emperor, he wants to be Kleagle.

—March 27, 1933

Italy has "black shirts,"[20] but no pants to go with them.

—October 16, 1930

Well, England and France, they're up there and they've told Russia, "Now, you're communistic, and you believe in dividing up everything." And they said, "Ordinarily, we don't believe in it. But it looks like we're going to have a war over here and we would like to split it with you boys."

So they're going to let Russia in on a good thing in case it shows up.

—March 31, 1935

In Europe public men do resign. But here it's a lost art. You have to impeach 'em.

—June 7, 1928

Every day we get new surprises from Europe. Sunday some fellow from Germany named Hess[21] who said he was speaking for Hitler, told France there wasn't any use of them fighting, and that they would like to make up, it all sounded so friendly that you started peeping under the bottom to see what was hid.

—July 9, 1934

> FRANCE COULD NOT **hate** US ANY MORE UNLESS WE **helped** 'EM OUT IN ANOTHER WAR.
>
> —Notes

It is the open season in Europe for grouse and Americans. They shoot the grouse and put them out of their miseries.

—August 10, 1926

Spain is trying to get a Republic. They think one is great. That shows
their ignorance.

—October 16, 1930

I would like to stay in Europe long enough to find some country that
don't blame America for everything in the world that's happened to
'em in the last fifteen years. The other day they had a prison mutiny
and so every paper said it was American Movies and American
influence that give their prisoners this unusual idea. The birth rate
is falling off in Europe, so I am going to get out of here before we
get blamed.

—January 28, 1932

The way we look at things, we think Alsace-Lorraine was the only
Country that was ever taken away from another Nation. Why, you
can't find a piece of ground in Europe that hasn't been taken at least
a dozen times from somebody or other that really think they have an
original claim to it.

—August 26, 1926

Take those little Balkan nations; they are like a little mess of stray
terriers. This is about the longest they have ever been between wars.

—October 19, 1930

I see where six members of the Greek Cabinet were executed today for negligence. I hope that will be a lesson to our Cabinet.

—Notes

Russia and Poland are always on the verge of war. I remember when I was over in both countries, why they were growling at each other like a couple of fat prima donnas on the same opera bill.

—October 19, 1930

Belgium is just an unfortunate country geographically. No country has it in for Belgium personally. They just like to use their grounds to fight on. It's really not a country, it's a Military Highway.

If I was Belgium, I would rent the country out to say, France and Germany, move out till they got through with it, and then come back and get it in shape for the next war.

—September 13, 1925

ASIA

WILL ROGERS WAS AN INVETERATE WORLD TRAVELER, from his first trip abroad in 1902 at the age of 23 until his death at 56 while on a round-the-world trip with Wiley Post.

In 1931, he took an extended trip through Asia, stopping in Tokyo, Mukden, Harbin, Dairen, Peking, Shanghai, Singapore, India, Baghdad, and Jerusalem. What he saw in his travels caused him to become one of the early voices calling attention to Japanese imperialist ambitions and the striking effectiveness of the Japanese military:

> These Japanese run their wars just like they do their trains—right on time. If they are billed to take a Town at ten o'clock on a certain day, if you want to see it taken you better be there at ten, for ten past ten they will be taking another one.

War broke out ten thirty on the night of September the eighteenth, and by nine o'clock the next morning the whole city of Mukden was in Japanese hands.

China has the biggest Arsenal in the World. Supposed to be held alone by 20,000 troops. Couple of truck loads of...Japanese—went up and took it over.

Now about this Korea....Here is the place where Japan just lost her head. She thought the more Country you own the bigger you was....Well, this Korea was right by Japan and woe be to a weak nation if they live by a strong one. They either got to play with 'em or join 'em. You see, in this Manchurian mess, if Japan had never taken Korea, you wouldn't hear so much complaining from the rest of the world now. But they point to Korea, and say, 'Manchuria will be another Korea.' It's the first Horse you steal that always is thrown up to you.

The Japanese run their wars just like they run their trains—right on time. All their soldiers are trained between wars, not after one starts.

You see, we have been lucky that way; all our wars have waited on us till we could get ready. But the Japanese figure that they may have one where the enemy won't wait. So when it is booked all the preliminaries have already been arranged; each soldier knows not only where he is to go, but knows practically who he is to shoot.

—March 12, 1932

Had dinner and long chat with Roosevelt in Honolulu. The President told me: "Will, don't jump on Japan, just keep them from jumping on us."

—August 12, 1934

ABOARD *SS EMPRESS OF RUSSIA*: I was told we would lose a day for no other reason than to make somebody's calendar come out even.

Well, we lost a day. We gained a typhoon. We lost a lifeboat and I lost my whole internal possessions. An Oklahoma prairie product like me has no business on the ocean when it's washing away lifeboats.

—November 27, 1931

Well here I am in Nippon, which means "sun." I have had very little trouble with the language. 'Course I don't know all the words, but I can carry on a pretty fair conversation with the three words I have: Nippon, Banzai, and they got a word "Ohio" which means hello or good morning.

Over home, Ohio means the difference between being elected President and being just another ex-candidate.

—March 5, 1932

Yesterday we lost a whole day, so the argument has come up: When is it back home. We not only don't know what hour it is back there but we don't know what day it is.

It's Sunday here, but they say it's only Saturday at home. Everything is cockeyed to us anyhow, for here we are traveling straight west to get to the Far East, Japan, the Land of the Rising Sun, where it sets.

—November 30, 1931

I wanted to get to see those Head Hunters you Filipinos all have in your Country; we have 'em over Home, but we call 'em Income Tax Collectors. And I did want to meet Aguinaldo.[22] I have always been an admirer of that old Hombre. We used to call him a Bandit. Any man is a Bandit if he is fighting opposite you and licking you most of the time; but if you are fighting against him, why, that's Patriotism. The difference between a Bandit and a Patriot is a good Press Agent.

—April 30, 1930

Won't it be wonderful if we ever live to see the day when any country can have its own revolution, and even a private and congenial war with a neighboring nation, without uninvited guests?

—September 8, 1930

If you folks in the Philippine Islands want your liberty, there is really no better way to get even with you than to give it to you. There is nothing that will cure a nation of wanting liberty, as to give it to 'em.

But if you can run your country, why, we can copy your style and maybe do a better job of running ours.

—April 30, 1932

Arrived in Japan Saturday, everything peaceful and fine. They want a bigger navy and I think I will let 'em have it, for they are going to build it anyway.

—August 12, 1934

The Japanese feel they were put on earth for a purpose, but the Chinese, he feels he was put here by mistake.

—March 12, 1932

The Japanese are mighty polite and nice, and want you to see and like their country. They got everything we've got and if they haven't, you show it to 'em and they will make it.

—January 17, 1932

As far as our trade is concerned, you can't force 'em to buy your goods. Japan has found out that any door is open to those that have the best product at the cheapest money. A manufacturer can sit in his office if his car is cheaper and better than any other, car dealers will come clear there to buy 'em.

—April 30, 1932

WE WILL STOP THESE FACTIONS FROM **fighting** AMONG EACH OTHER IF WE HAVE TO **kill** THEM TO DO IT.

—February 4, 1927

I can tell American Diplomacy what has caused this hate of us over there. It's our missionaries who have been trying to introduce "chop suey" into China.

China didn't mind them eating it there, but when they tried to call it a Chinese dish, that's what made them start shooting at us.

—May 15, 1927

You know, those chopsticks are really not so difficult. With just a little practice you can get so you can do quite a bit of gastronomical damage with 'em. I got so finally I could catch flies with mine.

—March 5, 1932

In China you get in power through an army. You ask: "How do you get votes with an army?" What do you mean "votes"? There has been nothing voted by the people of China since Genghis Khan called for a vote of confidence, but brother, he got it!

—April 2, 1932

What would we say if the Chinese was to send a gunboat up the Mississippi River? All they would have to say is: We are protecting our laundries in Memphis and St. Louis.

—February 6, 1927

If I had only stayed a couple of days, I would have had a better idea of China. The more you talk to, the more you see, and the less you know. Always dodge the "expert who lived in China and knows China."

The last man that knew China was Confucius, and he died feeling that he was becoming a little confused about 'em.

—December 30, 1931

I came up to Peking and I been looking at Walls and old Palaces till I am groggy. The Forbidden City—that's the way to attract attention to anything—call it "Forbidden" and you couldn't keep an American out of there with a meat ax.

Well, this wasn't forbidden any more than Palm Springs, but by calling it "Forbidden" they grabbed off the yokels, me included.

—March 19, 1932

Nobody is going to take China. China, even if they never shot a gun for the rest of their lives, is the most powerful country in the world. You could move the whole of Japan's seventy million into the very heart of China, and in seventy years there wouldn't be seventy Japanese left.

—April 30, 1932

I tell you what the Orient needs. Don't bring a lot of clothes. You can get anything here, toilet articles, cigarettes, shoes, Scotch, and all of America's standard equipment.

But for mercy's sake, bring a pillow with feathers in it. These out here are stuffed with rice, which wouldn't be so bad if they had cooked it first.

—December 22, 1931

The Chinese are the most fortunate nation in the world for they know that nothing that happens to 'em can possibly be worse than something that's already happened.

—April 2, 1932

IT NEVER **mattered** TO US WHO WAS PRESIDENT OF CHINA, ANYWAY, BECAUSE WE COULDN'T **pronounce** HIS NAME, WHOEVER HE WAS.

—November 20, 1927

Japan, China, and Korea, they all was run by what they called "Dynasties." You know what is a Dynasty? No? Well, then I can tell you better if you don't. It's when one Family, or one gang runs a country till they get thrown out on their ear. That's a Dynasty.

We, at home, have what they call the Republican and the Democratic Dynasties. The old rulers passed out at death, ours pass out when found out.

—March 12, 1932

The biggest difference between the Oriental and the Occidental is one looks into the past, where they know what happened; the other looks into the future where they don't know any more than a Weather Bureau Man.

—April 2, 1932

Voting, as we know it, just ain't done in up-to-date Chinese circles.

—April 2, 1932

The Chinese problem! We are always hearing about the Chinese problem. To the Chinese it's no problem. Then we found that they had some things to sell cheaper than the rest of the world, so that, naturally made them a problem.

—April 2, 1932

The Chinese are the only ones that have mastered Mass Production and Mass Distribution, too. They have arranged Wars, Famines, Droughts, Floods, and Disease so that it takes care of the surplus. Hundreds of millions have lived on the same farms for four thousand years. They can't overproduce anything—if they do, they eat it. If they don't produce it, they don't eat it. So you can't beat that for a balance of Production versus Consumption.

—April 2, 1932

In the old days in China the rulers promised 'em nothing and made good. But now they get promises, so you see yourself how much better off they are. No comparison to the old days.

I read some of the platforms that these new rulers get in on—Prosperity, Lower Taxes, Equal Rights for the Workingman, and Throw the Foreigners Out. Sounds like our 100 percent American pledges, don't it? Their pledges are fulfilled, too, just like ours.

—April 2, 1932

> ## RUSSIA IS **starving** HER OWN PEOPLE IN ORDER TO FEED **propaganda** TO THE REST OF THE WORLD.
> —October 16, 1930

What we ought to do is import some Chinese missionaries from over there to come and show us, not how to be saved but how to raise something every year on our land. We just got the missionary business turned around. We are the ones that need converting more than they do.

—April 10, 1927

I just found out who China is like. It's the Democrats at home. Individually they are smart, likeable, and efficient, but let two get together and they both want to be President.

Formed a new government at Nanking yesterday and nobody would let the other be head man, so they called it a committee-government. Now everybody is President.

There is a new idea for you Democrats!

—January 3, 1932

China is in a mess, not only again, but yet.

—October 16, 1930

No nation likes Russia, and they don't like Communism and all that, but they would use them in case a war come around.

—March 31, 1935

ENDNOTES

Presidents
[1] George Woodward Wickersham, was a New York attorney appointed by President Hoover in 1929 to investigate the federal jurisprudence system and the administration of laws.

Politics
[2] John Raskob, National Chairman of the Democratic Party.
[3] Henry Fletcher, former U.S. Ambassador to Italy.

Congress
[4] John Herbert Dillinger, infamous bank robber and murderer in the 1920s and 1930s.

Democrats and Republicans
[5] William Edgar Borah, Republican U.S. Senator from Idaho and Chairman of the Foreign Affairs Committee.

War and Peace
[6] Gerald Prentiss Nye, Republican U.S. Senator from North Dakota, was an Isolationist who had headed a senate committee investigating the role American arms manufacturers played in the U.S. entry into World War I.

Women
[7] Nineteenth Amendment to the U.S. Constitution, granting voting rights to American citizens of either gender.
[8] Eighteenth Amendment to the U.S. Constitution, prohibiting alcoholic beverages.
[9] Mabel Walker Willebrandt, Assistant U.S. Attorney General, well known for her support of Prohibition.

Education
[10] Nicholas Murray Butler, President of Columbia University from 1902 to 1945, presidential advisor, and recipient of the 1931 Nobel Peace Prize.

Crime and Law
[11] Alphonse "Scarface Al" Capone, foremost Chicago gangster of the 1920s and 1930s.

Labor
[12] Samuel Gompers, American labor leader and co-founder of the A.F. of L.

Holidays
[13] Worst catastrophic flood of the Mississippi River on record.
[14] Clara Bow was a Hollywood movie star, and the so-called "It" girl of the 1920s.

Latin America
[15] Augusto Cesar Sandino, a revolutionary, was captured by Nicaraguan National Guard and was executed February 21, 1934.
[16] Francisco (Pancho) Villa, a Mexican revolutionary, was assassinated 1923.
[17] Smith W. Brookhart, U.S. Senator from Iowa.

Europe
[18] Adolf Hitler, German dictator, 1933–1945.
[19] Benito Mussolini, Italian dictator, 1922–1943.
[20] "Black Shirts" were the official uniform of Mussolini's militia.
[21] Rudolf W.R. Hess, Adolf Hitler's second in command.

Asia
[22] Emilio Aguinaldo y Famy, 1869–1964, Filipino general and independence leader, considered first President of Philippines, 1899–1901.